COMIC
TO
CLASSICS

*A Parent's Guide
to Books for
Teens and Preteens*

Arthea J. S. Reed

University of North Carolina at Asheville

ira

INTERNATIONAL READING ASSOCIATION
Newark, Delaware 19714

Copyright 1988 by the
International Reading Association, Inc.

Library of Congress Cataloging in Publication Data

Reed, Arthea J.S.
    Comics to classics: A parent's guide to books for teens and preteens / Arthea (Charlie) Reed.
        p. cm.
    Bibliography: p.
        1. Teenagers—Books and reading. 2. Children—Books and reading. 3. Reading—Parent participation. 4. Young adult literature—Bibliography. 5. Children's literature—Bibliography. 6. Youth—Books and reading. I. International Reading Association. II. Title.
    Z1037.A1R428 1988   028.1'625055—dc19   88-10171
    ISBN 0-87207-798-5

Contents

PART THREE   Sharing Books

PART FOUR   Locating Books

PART FIVE   Appendix

Graphic design by Larry Husfelt
Cover photograph by Mary Lowenstein-Anderson
Photo credits: Mary Lowenstein-Anderson pages 6, 10, 16, 20, 25, 62, 80, 88,
    100, 105, 113; Martha Brown pages 2, 9, 13, 29; Norman Prince page 96.

To my parents, Martha and Fred Staeger,
who encouraged my love of books.

Foreword

I f you are reading these words, chances are you are either interested in or concerned about your child as a reader. Welcome to the club.

While membership in this "club" is informal and open to anyone, it is somewhat "exclusive." Exclusive in the unfortunate sense that potential members keep excluding themselves, preferring instead to join shopping clubs, sports clubs, television clubs, and video clubs. Reading, they mistakenly guess, would take too much time and energy. And besides, children's reading is the domain of teachers. As a parent, what do I know about reading?

That depends on how much you *want* to know. If you finish reading this book, you'll know a lot more about children and their reading than you knew before.

The first thing you need to know is that you are a member of the largest and most important teacher corps in the world—you are a parent. Everything that keeps us civilized, everything that is truly important, is taught by parents: how to live, how to love, and even how to work. This is accomplished largely through example and imitation.

For more reasons than biological, I am a parent because my parents were. As a child, I liked what I saw happening in my home and decided to do likewise in my own home. I am a reader for the same reason. I saw and heard my parents reading every day. Must be important, I thought, and so began my life as a reader. Although occasional exceptions do surface, it's safe to say that readers raise readers.

Let's assume for the moment you have done all the right things up to this point: Your child has seen and heard you reading; there are books, magazines, and newspapers in the home; and everyone in the family owns a library card. We might even safely say your child enjoys reading. Now your child approaches the rocky shoals of adolescence. As his or her appetite, hair, skin, voice, clothes, friends, and taste in music begin to suffer dramatic changes, you are worried the child's reading appetite will change. Rest assured it will. But you have much to do with whether it changes for better or worse.

If you haven't replaced the books your child read in fifth grade, if your weekly trip to the library has become a monthly one, and if you find the family returning more borrowed videos than borrowed books, please note these are danger signs, signaling a negative turn in reading.

Keep in mind that reading—like riding a bicycle—is an acquired skill. The more you read, the better you read; and the better you read, the more you like reading. Conversely, the less you read, the less you enjoy reading. Therefore, the trick is to keep a child reading through adolescence.

The environment you create or promote in your home is important. Is there a reading lamp beside your child's bed? Do you include magazine subscriptions and books among the gifts you give your child? Is there a plentiful supply of reading material in the family room, bedroom, bathroom, and kitchen? Most important, do you lead by example? Does your child see you reading? And if so, what do you read? One of the best things you can do to raise a reader through adolescence is to read adolescent literature. If you have never read teen or preteen literature, it will both surprise and please you and some of it will challenge, even *provoke* you. But until you have read adolescent literature, you will never be able to enthuse over it or discuss it. Your child may figure you don't care, and if you're not interested, why should he or she be.

Arthea (Charlie) Reed's compilation of titles and annotations is a wonderful guide through the forest of young adult literature, not just for parents but for anyone who cares about adolescents—aunts, uncles, coaches, librarians, teachers and, obviously, students themselves.

Most of us know the books teenagers hate. Some of us still have scar tissue from when they were forced down our throats in junior and senior high school—the books that seemed to specialize in turning readers *off* instead of turning them *on*. (I suspect there were English department chairs who mistakenly rationalized: "Since reading dies in most people by age 19, we'd better squeeze in Shakespeare and Thomas Hardy before it's too late." Didn't they ever wonder *why* reading died?) In any case, you'll find none of those books here. Here are the books that keep young readers reading, thinking, enjoying, and sharing with one another.

Few things sustain a culture as well as reading. It could even lead to the day when you will find passengers on planes reading instead of sleeping!

JIM TRELEASE

Introduction

Through literature I become a thousand [people] and
yet remain myself.

C.S. Lewis

Recently, the father of a ten year old asked me, "What happened to Dr. Spock? Why did he stop giving me advice just when I needed him most?"

This question has been echoed by many parents. When our children are infants, toddlers, and in elementary school, advice is abundant about everything from rashes to reading. But when they reach the preteen and teenage years, help is practically nonexistent.

The concern of this father is not new. I remember my grandmother's warning to my mother, "When the children are little, they are little problems; when they are big, they are big problems." From this distant memory and this father's question comes the inspiration for this book.

At best, adolescence* is a time of change, of transition from the toys of childhood to the responsibilities of adulthood. At worst, it is a time of torment. We may remember our own adolescence with pain or nostalgia, and we experience our children's adolescence with fear, frustration, and empathy.

As a youth, books provided me great solace. I laughed and cried with the sisters in Louisa May Alcott's *Little Women*. I experienced the excitement of besting my elders while solving a mystery with Nancy Drew. I felt the love and pain of Angie in Maureen Daly's *Seventeenth Summer*. I created in my mind's eye the land of Narnia and celebrated the defeat of evil in C.S. Lewis' *The Chronicles of Narnia*. Through the literature of my youth, I lived the lives of the young women and men who populated the pages of my books. I defeated dragons; I found the love of wonderfully kind and

---

*The young people discussed in this book are between the ages of 10 and 20. They are referred to as preadolescents, adolescents, young adults, preteens, or teens.

supportive young men; I solved problems of hidden staircases and lost jewels; I belly laughed; and I cried from the heart. And all the while I remained myself. The characters in my books taught me not to fear the world. They taught me that life can be hard, even tragic. They also taught me that faith, wisdom, and love can defeat the world's evils. Even on the worst days of my adolescence I believed this, and I still believe it.

My parents encouraged my love of books. They rarely complained when I spent an entire lazy day reading a book. In fact, they let my friend Alyce and me spend an entire summer reading books under the apple tree in our backyard. For that, and for the many other things they taught me, I dedicate this book to them, with love. I also dedicate it to all the parents who know the magic of books and care so deeply for their adolescent children that they want to share the magic with them.

Because I believe that the best way to understand books for adolescents is to understand adolescents, I begin the book with them. The first three chapters discuss the stages of adolescent development. Parents can read the chapters most appropriate for the ages of their adolescent children. I hope these chapters will begin to answer the father's cry for help that began this introduction.

Chapter 4 talks about the adolescent as a reader. Unfortunately, many adolescents are not motivated to read; even if they are motivated to read, they can't find books they want to read. The chapter explains why and gives parents some helpful suggestions.

Chapters 5 through 7 are the heart of the book; they are about the books adolescents read. Chapter 5 discusses the wide variety of books for adolescents. Chapters 6 and 7 list books, give brief plot summaries of each, provide an appropriate age range, and discuss other elements of books that might be of interest to parents.

Chapters 8 and 9 are designed to help parents share books with adolescents. They discuss techniques parents can use to encourage their adolescents to read and examine the value of discussing books with adolescents.

Chapters 10 through 12 help parents locate appropriate books for their adolescent children. Chapter 13 gives parents additional sources for finding out more about adolescence and how to deal with its specific problems.

Writing this book has been a work of love, a work inspired by the many wonderful parents I know; the adolescent I was; the books I remember; the wonderful authors who write of adolescence; and the adolescents who share with me their "energy, enthusiasm, confusion, hope, despair, love, optimism, faith, and belief."

I hope this book will help you bring the magic of books to the adolescents in your life.

Arthea (Charlie) Reed

X

PART ONE

Teens and Preteens

*T*he land of the young is the land of energy, enthusiasm, confusion, hope, despair, love, optimism, faith, and belief.

Norma Fox Mazer

The Preadolescent and Reading

The Preadolescent

Preadolescence is a time when a child is no longer a child but not yet an adult. It is an in-between, difficult time that is hard to define in terms of age. Maturation begins at different times and continues at different rates in different individuals.

A seventh grade classroom is a good place to observe the differences in physical, social, emotional, and intellectual maturity in young people who are about the same age. Judy, who is 12.5 years old, is physically mature but acts like a child. Frank, at four feet seven inches and almost 13 years old, answers questions with the maturity of an adult. Barbara, 12.4 years, not only looks mature, but acts mature, at least socially. She spends an entire class period making eyes at Jim. Jim, 12.8 years, also is physically mature, but, unlike Barbara, he has no interest in the opposite sex. He has the latest copy of *Sports Illustrated* in his desk and reads it whenever he gets a chance.

Who are these young people? How will they change in the next few years? What are their reading interests today, and what will they read next year and the year after?

All of these young people are adolescents. Some are in the midst of puberty; others have not left childhood. For all of them, it is a time of physical change and intense involvement with peers.

Physical Development and Attachment to Peers

By late childhood (ages 10-13), children are experiencing significant physical change. Psychologist Robert Havighurst explains that this change can cause hyperactivity, rebelliousness, moodiness, and irritability, and it can diminish self-confidence just when preadolescents are striving to build it.

One of my favorite pastimes is watching young people at a local swimming pool. Since I see many of these young people only at the pool, the physical changes I observe when the pool opens in June can be startling. Consider a group of girls I watched recently. The summer before, they had been children who were constantly active, jumping out of the pool, climbing the ladder, and jumping off the high dive. Their legs were skinny and their chests were flat. In one year incredible physical and social changes had occurred. All but one had grown several inches and all were beginning to look like young women.

Their behavior had changed too. No longer did they shout across the pool to their mothers. Now they wanted to be seen only with their peers. Two of the girls arrived at the pool carrying large radios. They all had nearly identical beach bags stocked with coconut oil, brushes, and beach towels. They found several lounge chairs directly across from the lifeguard and set up shop. I observed them for nearly two hours, and not one of them got wet.

I was not sure of the girls' ages, but they appeared to be about 12. Like most young people that age, they rarely sat still. Though their towels remained on the chairs, the girls were on the move. In two hours I counted three trips to the soda machine, four walks around the perimeter of the pool, two trips to the water fountain, countless trips to the restroom, and two trips to the telephone. None of the girls traveled alone.

The physical differences in the girls' maturation clearly influenced their self-confidence. One of them had developed far more than her peers, and she obviously found this embarrassing. Every time she got up to visit friends or to run to the soda machine, she put an oversized blouse over her bathing suit. Another girl had matured little since the previous summer; she sat with a towel draped around her one piece suit.

The girls' interactions with their mothers also had changed. Late in the afternoon, one of the mothers came to pick them up. The previous year they had darted repeatedly from the pool to mother's beach chair; now they practically ignored her. She walked over to their chairs, said a few words to them (which they tried to ignore), moved away to talk to a friend, and finally began calling to them impatiently. As they slowly packed their gear, they never acknowledged her presence.

Change Affects Both Sexes

Boys, too, find it difficult to deal with the physical changes of adolescence. Rapid growth can make it almost impossible for boys to sit still, so they often appear to be hyperactive and clumsy. These traits make it difficult for boys to function in a cramped classroom.

Probably the most humiliating change for young men is voice change, which usually occurs during the preadolescent years. Jeff Garrett, a character in Lois Duncan's *Killing Mr. Griffin*, remembers the embarrassment (p. 24).

> He remembered the first time they met each other. Jeff had been twelve then, big for his age, standing head and shoulders above the others in the seventh-grade classroom. He had felt huge and self-conscious. His voice had already been starting to change. When roll was called he answered with a froglike croak, and the rest of the class had burst into laughter.
>
> Even the teacher had smiled, and Jeff had felt the sting of hot tears in his eyes. He had blinked them back, furious at himself, hating all of them. Choking on his own fury, he had wedged himself into the seat behind the desk, wishing he could disappear beneath it.

The Preadolescent Reader

For many young adults, the peak of reading interest occurs around age 12. By then, most preadolescents can read comfortably a wide range of materials on a variety of reading levels. When young readers enter middle or junior high school, they are no longer learning to read in the sense of learning to gain basic meaning from the written word. Instead, they are "reading to learn."

Expanding Interests

By the time preadolescents are 12, their interests have expanded beyond the neighborhood and school. They are curious about many things. However, they have limited capabilities for exploring their widening world. Most preadolescents are limited by how far they can walk or pedal, how far the bus or subway goes, or how far their parents are willing to drive them. Most have limited funds and are restricted by parental regulations. Much of their interest and curiosity must be satisfied by television, movies, and books.

How Reading Skills Develop

Reading is a skill that develops slowly. It is probably true that some people have a natural ability that makes it easier for them to read. Likewise, some people grow up in environments that allow them to develop reading skills with ease and enjoyment. However, it is also true that most young people are capable of learning to read. Bruno

Bettelheim and Karen Zelan say that if young readers are allowed to develop reading skills naturally, in supportive environments, and without undue pressure, they are likely to become readers by the time they leave elementary school.

Like most other skills, reading develops in stages. Educator Margaret Early explains that the earliest stage of reading development begins long before children can identify letters or words. She calls this period the stage of "unconscious enjoyment," which begins during the preschool years and continues until preadolescence. During this time, children love to play with words, to hear words repeated, to make rhymes and riddles, to sing, and to create nonsense words and sentences. According to Early, this love of language and the ability to play with words fortifies children as they struggle to learn to read. Children who have not discovered the joy of language may experience difficulty in learning to read, since learning to read requires playing with language and trying out new sounds, techniques, and words. Parents should encourage this playfulness in their preadolescent children.

Conclusion

This period of transition from childhood to young adulthood can be trying for preadolescents and their parents. However, if their homes provide a comfortable place of refuge, preadolescents are likely to continue to look upon the family as a source of comfort and protection while seeking new roles in their ever expanding world. If, as parents, we help our youngsters capitalize on the energy, enthusiasm, hope, love, optimism, faith, and belief of youth and minimize their confusion and despair, they should pass through these years with relative ease.

Chapter 2

*D*uring adolescence we encounter the most deeply
felt things in life—love, fear of rejection, death
perhaps, and intense happiness. We often
respond with greater emotion than at any other point in our
lives. Adolescence is often a worrisome period of pressures—
pressure to do well in school, to gain acceptance from
friends, to cope with problems without the benefit of experience that adults often take for granted.

Kevin Major

The Early Adolescent
and Reading

The Early Adolescent

Early adolescence, between the ages of 13 and 15, is marked by rapid growth and
physical development. Youngsters in this age group often are restless and rebellious.
According to Margaret A. Edwards, author of *The Fair Garden and the Swarm of
Beasts: The Library and the Young Adult*, "the adolescent is bound by confusion and
bewilderment in his attempts to find out who he is and what identity to assume. He
needs to know others who have been under the same constraints and have freed
themselves....As he matures, the young person wants to break out of his shell and
become involved with others. He wants to be free from the narrow confines of self
and find meaning for his life." Early adolescents establish relationships with peers,
first of the same sex and later of the opposite sex. In addition, they begin to seek their

own identity within the conformity of the peer group. This causes potential for conflict between peers and family and can result in personal identity problems and changed relationships with parents.

Peer Group and Family: A Potential Conflict

The move toward the peer group and away from the family often leads to conflict and sometimes rebellion. By early adolescence the peer group is the most important source for social affection; the family can no longer meet this need.

Adolescent peer groups usually require conformity to the dress, speech, interests, and values of the group. At times, these conflict with the standards of individuals and their families, causing problems between parents and adolescents. Early adolescents, to whom peer group membership and independence from the family are of prime importance, often select group membership rather than conform to the wishes of the family.

Peer Group and Personal Identity: A Potential Conflict

Even while conforming to the peer group, early adolescents begin to seek a personal identity. It is not unusual to hear junior high or early high school students say "I want to be accepted for who I am." But, "who I am" often is dictated by the peer group. This is a potential conflict for early adolescents.

Early adolescents also begin to establish new relationships at home. They want increased freedom from parents and rules. They are likely to develop opinions that reflect those of the peer group and express them freely. Early adolescents may change the way they dress and seek more freedom to decide with whom to spend time and when, where, and how often. They start looking for new ways of getting money, recognizing that money leads to increased independence. This pull away from the family can lead to conflict, and unresolved conflict can lead to rebellion.

On the other hand, early adolescents often fear their new independence and seek support from the family. They may fight against rules, but they often find constraints comforting.

We do not know why some early adolescents have little difficulty progressing through these years, while others are overwhelmed by conflicting goals and values. We do know, however, that early adolescents must establish new relationships with peers and family and at the same time establish a new identity for themselves.

The Egocentric Early Adolescent Reader

By the time they are early adolescents, youngsters have progressed to what Margaret Early refers to as the egocentric stage of reading development. This stage corresponds with the adolescent's struggle for peer acceptance and personal identity. Even in selecting reading material, early adolescents seek to meet these egocentric needs.

Becoming a Reader

By late junior high or early senior high school, teenagers can read independently and are willing to exert some effort on reading. However, if reading a book requires too much effort, readers are likely to become frustrated and quit reading. If they are frustrated too often, they may quit reading altogether. This is understandable when we consider that early adolescents need to be in control of their own lives. If books constantly defeat youngsters and make them feel inferior, they are likely to quit reading. It is less embarrassing to quit reading than to feel inadequate.

Parents must be aware of this problem. Many parents would like their children to read the classics, but most early adolescents are neither emotionally nor intellectually mature enough to meet the demands of these books. If we force books on our children, they may quit reading entirely. However, if we help them find appropriate books, they are likely to become avid readers.

Establishing an Identity through Books

Adolescents can use books to help establish their own identities. It is important for early adolescent readers to see themselves in the characters, plots, and themes of the books they read. If readers find stories unbelievable, characters unrealistic, or themes obscure, they are likely to call the book "boring" or "dumb" and to discard it. If they do continue reading (perhaps because the book is required), it will be read painfully. Herein lies another danger. Youngsters who frequently read books that do not meet their egocentric needs may decide that all books are a waste of time. Therefore, when we suggest books to early adolescents, we should seek books with young characters who deal with the realistic concerns of adolescents.

Characters Must Live Adolescence

Able readers at this stage of development also face another danger. Adults enjoy nostalgic books about adolescence that look at these years in retrospect. Adolescents, however, are living their youth. Many retrospective books appear to young readers to speak down to them and to preach. Adolescents are put off by these books, in spite of the fact that the characters are young. Parents cannot assume that because a book has a young character it is appropriate for young egocentric readers. Characters must be living through adolescence, not looking back on it.

Parents Can Provide Guidance

It is during this stage of egocentric reading development that parents can provide significant help and guidance. Without the help of parents, adolescents frequently quit reading. The books adolescents are required to read in school rarely relate to their needs and interests; they reflect the world of adult literature. Consequently, it is especially important that books they read for pleasure meet their needs for peer acceptance and the establishment of a personal identity. Parents who know

Early adolescent readers enjoy books with realistic teenage characters.

their adolescent children and who are acquainted with young adult literature* can introduce their youngsters to books that will meet their needs and help them become mature adult readers.

Conclusion

Early adolescence is a period of potential conflict both within adolescents and between adolescents and adults. It is also an exciting time in which the restless energy of the teenager can be put to positive use. It is a time in which adolescents are willing to exert effort not only in the area of reading, but in the areas of personal development, interpersonal relationships, and social problems. Many young people grow into thinking, caring young adults during this period. Though parents may feel they have little influence on their teenagers, the examples they provide and the understanding they exhibit allow their relationships with their adolescents to mature.

---

*Young adult literature is literature written for and read by adolescents aged 10 to 12. It is also called adolescent literature and juvenile literature.

Chapter 3

(Speaking to adolescent readers)

I *want to give you a glimpse of the choices you have before you, of the price that will be asked of you....When you know what life has to sell, for how much, and what it can give away free, you will not live in darkness. I hope that in books you'll find your light, and that by this light you may cross from one shore of love to another, from your childhood into your adulthood.*

Maia Wojciechowska

The Late Adolescent and Reading

The Late Adolescent

The late adolescent, between the ages of 15 and 18, looks like an adult and wants to be treated as an adult, but lacks the experience, wisdom, and maturity of adulthood. Growth slows down during this period. Most girls of 16 and boys of 18 have reached their full physical growth.

Social Affection versus Self-Esteem

Many late adolescents are still striving to achieve social affection, particularly those who are not members of a peer group of their choice. However, more are struggling to meet the need of self-esteem as they maintain the social affection of the peer group. Unfortunately, these two needs are often in conflict.

At times young people seeking social affection may select a path to peer group membership that conflicts with family values. Therefore, acceptance by the group will not lead to self-esteem, but to frustration. For example, if the peer group uses alcohol or drugs and the family does not, the young person will face a conflict of values. When values are in conflict, self-esteem is not possible.

On the other hand, a path that is acceptable to the family may be unpopular with the chosen peer group. For example, a young adult whose family is associated with a particular religious faith may be an outsider in the peer group. Young adult author Norma Fox Mazer writes of this from her own experience: "I was a girl, but not an 'in' girl. I had too many strikes against me: I lived on the wrong side of town. I was Jewish. I had opinions. I didn't know how to make small talk or flirt. I didn't have a steady boyfriend. I was 'serious,' as well, with political ideas. None of these gave me status." So, Mazer turned to books and, eventually, to writing to find acceptance.

Too Many Questions

Late adolescents are required to answer many adult questions before they are ready. Will I seek additional education? Will I get a job? Will I quit school? Will I go steady? Will I get married? Will I maintain the values of my family or develop my own values? These questions can produce conflict for young adults and their families. It is difficult for parents to provide answers to these questions. Late adolescents view themselves as mature and independent, and in many ways they are. Adolescents often shut out their parents, viewing them as symbols of childhood dependence. Adolescents who continue to read may find help in books to answer their difficult questions.

The Late Adolescent Reader

Late adolescents who read for pleasure are well on the road to becoming mature, adult readers. They are willing to exert considerable effort in reading and to tackle increasingly challenging books. At times they will take on particularly difficult books simply to meet the challenge.

The Joy of Reading

When maturing readers are willing to read almost anything, Margaret Early says they have entered the aesthetic stage of reading. Aesthetic readers read for the joy of reading and to meet a variety of purposes: for pleasure, to gain general knowledge, to locate specific information, to learn more about a topic, to learn a new skill. They are likely to be reading several books at one time. According to Early's studies, the aesthetic stage is rarely reached before the late high school years; often it is never reached. Recent statistics that show the average adult in the United States reads only

11

1.2 books per year confirm this. If readers are to reach the aesthetic stage, they must pass through the egocentric stage with minimal difficulty. If they skip a stage, they are unlikely to progress to the next stage of reading development.

Egocentric Needs Still Present

Most late adolescents still select books that meet their egocentric needs, with young characters and realistic plots. We can continue to suggest these books to them. Look for books with characters who are a year or two older than the reader and who are beginning to face increasingly adult problems. As teenagers' interests begin to broaden, we can suggest a wider range of books on more adult topics.

It is important to note that maturing readers can be at more than one stage of reading development at a time. It is possible, for example, for young adults to continue to read books with young characters and simple, straightforward plots while beginning to tackle more difficult works of literature.

Conclusion

The period of late adolescence is the final bridge from childhood to adulthood. Books written by skilled authors can help adolescents pose and answer some of the most compelling questions of young adulthood.

Chapter 4

*T*he things young people want to read are related to
their chronological age regardless of the level of their
reading ability. Even if they have one foot in the
world of adult literature, one foot will remain in the literature
of childhood. I remember that one of my daughters, the summer
before she reached sixteen, not only read War and Peace—at
that time I had not read it— but also Maureen Daly's Seventeenth Summer.

Jeannette H. Eyerly

Encouraging Teens
and Preteens to Read

Why Good Readers Quit Reading

The peak of reading interest often occurs around age 12; that is also the age when
many readers lose interest in books. This happens for several reasons. Young readers
are required by schools or pushed by parents to read books for which they are not
emotionally and intellectually ready. Many adolescents have difficulty finding books
with young characters who face the problems of adolescence. Some parents, teachers,
and librarians are unaware of appropriate books to recommend. Some adults discourage adolescents from selecting books on certain topics or themes of interest. (One

mother limits her teenage daughter's reading to books with "happy endings." Not surprisingly, the girl rarely reads.) For some adolescents, reading is not accepted by their peer group.

What Parents Can Do to Keep Adolescents Reading

If we are aware of these stumbling blocks and understand our adolescent's ego-centric reading interests, we can encourage the beginning of mature, aesthetic reading patterns. There are several things we can do: Make reading fun, never push, and encourage a wide range of reading interests.

Help make reading fun. For example, we must remember that preadolescents need to play with language, and we should encourage books in which language is fun. Joke books are often a good bridge to higher levels of reading development. Comic books serve the same function for some youngsters. Parents shouldn't discourage pre-adolescents from reading these books. Instead, we can help our preteenagers broaden this interest by suggesting humorous young adult books like Paula Danziger's *The Cat Ate My Gymsuit,* which is particularly appropriate for preteenage girls, or Roald Dahl's *Charlie and the Chocolate Factory.* Many of the books listed in Chapter 6 relate to the preadolescent's interests and needs and include playful use of language.

Never push. Don't push young readers beyond what they are willing to tackle. Many girls are interested in romance. Parents should not discourage this interest. In fact, we can encourage it by suggesting some young adult romances of high literary quality. (Most of the "love and romance" books discussed in Chapter 6 fall into this category.) This keeps girls reading and at the same time helps them mature in their literary tastes. To help broaden adolescents' reading interests, we should look carefully at the books they select. For example, readers who read romances may have enjoyed several Gothic romance novels. These books are set in another time, in a distant land, and contain many of the literary conceits of mystery novels. We might help these readers broaden their reading interests by introducing them to young adult historical fiction and mystery. (Books in all of these genres are suggested in Chapter 6.)

Encourage a wide range of reading interests. Parents should encourage a wide range of reading interests in teenagers. Many of us praise our children when they select adult, classic works, but we say little or even criticize them when they select young adult books. It is important to remember that the aesthetic reader, who is becoming a mature adult reader, has a broad range of reading interests. The young adult who reads a Judy Blume novel over the weekend, picks up *Gone with the Wind* in the library on Monday, and reads *Seventeen* magazine that evening is becoming an aesthetic reader. We should encourage all of these reading interests.

Encouraging Reluctant Readers

Unfortunately, some adolescents rarely read, not because they can't but because they won't. Some quit reading altogether. These reluctant readers are unlikely to develop mature, aesthetic reading patterns; they are likely to become nonreading adults.

Why Some Young People Dislike Reading

A study by Lance Gentile and Merna McMillan can help us understand why some young people who are capable of reading well are reluctant to read. That understanding can provide parents with some clues as to how to deal with teenagers who dislike reading.

Many adolescents equate reading with ridicule, failure, or exclusively school related tasks. If this is true of your adolescent, you can help by providing an example that reading is fun. Parents who read for pleasure are more likely to have children who read for pleasure. Encourage nonreading adolescents to purchase magazines in areas that interest them. Be sure your youngster sees you reading magazines. Buy paperback books and read them. When you purchase a book, ask if your teenager would like to buy one too. It is important to remember that the only way to get out of the nonreading habit is to read. Don't push adolescents into books they are unwilling to tackle; encourage them to read magazines or books they will enjoy and make such reading material available.

Some people are not excited by ideas. Many adolescents are driven to experience life directly, rather than through reading. Social interaction is one of teenagers' most basic needs, and it is difficult to interact socially while reading a book. Adults need to help adolescents see that books can make life more exciting. For example, if your son and his friends plan to go white water rafting, you can purchase a book on the topic or check one out of the library for him. Perhaps he will begin to see that reading about the experience can enhance his enjoyment of it.

A great number of adolescents do not want to sit, and in some cases are incapable of sitting, for prolonged periods. Adolescence is one of the most physically active periods of life. Parents, particularly of youngsters just entering puberty, should keep this in mind when selecting or suggesting reading material. Magazines are good for young adolescents since the articles are short and are aimed at the egocentric reading needs of teenagers. Most young adult books have short chapters that begin with "hooks" to force the reader to keep reading and end with "clinchers" to make the reader turn to the next chapter.

Adolescence is a time of intense egocentrism. Young adult literature encourages teenagers to keep reading. Unfortunately, most literature programs in middle, junior, and senior high schools do not encourage the reading of young adult books. In fact, many of these programs require the reading of classics that are often far removed from the egocentric needs of young readers. These programs, designed to develop mature readers, often keep adolescents from becoming mature readers by ignoring their egocentric stage of reading development. Parents can help by introducing adolescents to young adult books. (Chapters 6 and 7 are designed to help you do so.)

Many young people demand to be entertained. Young adult books should solve the problem of the "boring" book. Young adults demand entertainment, and young adult books provide it.

Encourage a wide range of reading interests by allowing teenagers to select their own reading materials.

Many students are pressured to read. It is difficult for parents and teachers to encourage young people to read without pressuring them. The line between the two is thin, but encouragement has some characteristics that help to distinguish it from pressure. In an encouraging atmosphere, a wide variety of reading material is available. Adolescents are allowed to select their own reading materials. Parents and teachers are aware of the adolescents' interests and needs and seek books addressing these. Young adult books are readily available. Adults pay more attention to the fact that youngsters are reading than to what they are reading.

Many young people grow up in an atmosphere where there is no reading material, but it's never too late to change the environment. Inexpensive books can be purchased at used bookstores; library cards usually are free. Children model their parents' actions; if we read, children are likely to read.

Reading is considered antisocial by many adolescents, particularly if the teenager is part of a nonreading peer group. This may be the hardest trend to reverse. Parents can help by attempting to discover acceptable reading material. Sometimes magazines or comic books are of interest to the peer group when books are not. Some teenagers are more willing to accept paperback books than hardcover books, which may look too much like textbooks. Paperback publishers work hard to develop covers that appeal to adolescents. Adolescents who rarely read are most likely to be attracted to covers that are realistic and similar to magazine covers. Another way to get teenagers to read is to select material that relates to peer group interest. If the peer group is interested in cars, try to find books about cars and auto mechanics. A youngster who learns about cars through books may become more acceptable to the peer group.

Some adolescents view reading as part of the adult world and reject it. For some adolescents, anything that appears to be adult is unacceptable. This problem usually decreases as the young person grows older. If your teenager always has been a reader, if your house is filled with books, and if you read, it is likely your youngster will grow into a reader. Parents must avoid pushing; the more we push teenagers toward books, the more they will run from them.

Helping Teens Who Can't Read

If your teenager is a poor reader, it is even more urgent that you get him or her to read. This will be more difficult because your child has been defeated by books, but it is more important because the only way to improve reading skills is to read.

Techniques That Work (Sometimes)

As a teacher of adolescents, I've tried all kinds of techniques with teenagers who don't read because they can't read. I've shown them studies that prove that the better people read, the more they earn over a lifetime. I've tried to teach reading through learning to read the driver's manual and income tax forms. I've asked students to level with me: "Why can't you read? You're smart. What happened?" I have had success with all of these techniques, but the success has been limited to a few individuals.

I sympathize with parents of adolescents who face this problem. Nothing is more frustrating than trying to convince someone to do something when that person is convinced that he or she knows better than you, particularly when that person is your adolescent child. I also understand all the reasons why these poor readers resist learning to read; I am not so different myself. I know I cannot rollerskate, so don't suggest a rollerskating party; I won't go. Like many adolescents, I'd rather fail by not trying, so I can justify my defeat by saying, "I didn't want to go anyway. Rollerskating is dumb, and it's dangerous to my health." Poor readers are very good at justifying their failure when they don't try, but unfortunately that does not solve their problem. In the end, they still can't read.

Admitting the problem is the first step. I can only imagine how difficult the problem is for parents, but perhaps I can use my experience as a teacher to offer some encouragement. Honesty is the first step toward helping youngsters tackle their reading problems. They have to admit they cannot read, or at least not well. I usually begin by asking them to tell me about their reading experiences. What is it about reading that makes it so difficult? I avoid preaching or judging. I try to understand their problems. (It helps to remember that there are many things I cannot and will not do.)

Discussing the problem. By discussing the problem, we've admitted that it exists. Many young people, once they've admitted that not being able to read is a problem, are willing to try to improve their reading skills. I let them know it will not be easy. I encourage them and express my appreciation for even the smallest achievement. Learning to read is very difficult; it is more difficult for young adults than it is for children. Many young adults no longer experience the unconscious enjoyment children find in playing with language. For them, there is little except humiliation in the process.

Getting help. If you have an adolescent with a severe reading problem, get help. Going through the process described above with your own child is almost impossible; a tutor can help. Many communities provide free tutoring for adolescents and adults. Usually, the principal or guidance counselor in your child's school can help you find a tutoring service.

Finding materials for poor readers. A major difficulty for parents with teenagers who do not read well is finding material they can read that is not too juvenile. Within the field of young adult literature there is a classification known as high interest-easy reading. This material is designed to be easy to read, but to appeal to the maturity level of the young adult. Books in this classification appear with an asterisk in Chapters 6 and 7.

Conclusion

By preadolescence, most readers are capable of reading independently. The peak of their interest in reading often occurs around age 12. Young adolescents use reading to help achieve social acceptance. Books often provide teenagers with answers to perplexing concerns and questions.

Adolescence is also the time when many readers, even capable ones, quit reading. Parents who understand why adolescents don't read may be able to encourage their teenagers to continue reading by making available the right reading material at the right time.

PART TWO
Books for Teens and Preteens

Chapter 5

Y oung adult literature is transitional literature. By its
nature, it should move the reader closer to maturity
and not only by its subject matter and philosophy, but
also by its inventiveness of style, its characterization, sensitivity
and discovery, and most of all, by the commitment of its writers
to do their best work.

Sue Ellen Bridgers

The Teenager's World of Books

What Is Young Adult Literature?

G. Robert Carlsen says that young adult literature (also called adolescent or juvenile literature) is best defined as literature read by young adults. In other words, young adult literature includes books written specifically for adolescents as well as for children, adults, or a general audience. While it is true that adolescents read all kinds of books, there is a body of literature with specific characteristics that make it particularly appropriate for adolescents.

Though not all young adult books are alike, they have a number of common characteristics: simple plots, characters who are young or who experience situations of the young, stories told from the viewpoint of young characters, stories that never talk down to adolescents, modern themes that relate to the lives of young readers, chapter beginnings and endings that keep readers turning pages, mature format in terms of shape of the book and spareness of pictures, easy to read text (short chapters, clear type, more white space), simplicity of language, eye catching covers.

It is important to emphasize that "simple" does not mean less artistic or less literary. The best adolescent literature is as literary as the best adult literature.

What to Look for in Books for Young Adults

In general, books for young adults should have the following characteristics:

Characters
- A main character approximately one to two years older than the reader.
- A limited number of characters.
- Well developed characters who reach mature understanding by the end of the novel.
- Well developed, realistic relationships among central characters.

Plot
- Simple and fast moving.
- Realistic problems and conflicts.

Format
- Easy to read text, short chapters, clear type, more white space than adult books.
- Adult appearance.

Theme
- Themes that challenge young readers to question and think.

Point of View
- Stories that avoid talking down to readers or preaching, told from the viewpoint of the young adult protagonist.

Writing Style
- Tight, simple, lively language.
- Limited descriptions.
- Good, honest writing by an author who cares about adolescents.

Books for the Stages of Adolescent Development

Books for adolescents parallel the three stages of adolescent development identified by Robert Havighurst: Preadolescence (ages 10-13), early adolescence (ages 13-15), and late adolescence (ages 15-18). Books must reflect teenagers' interests and concerns, and since adolescents' needs change rapidly the maturity of books must grow with them. As parents, we are concerned with helping our youngsters select books appropriate for their level of maturity. Chapters 6 and 7 list hundreds of books for adolescents with an appropriate age range indicated for each.

Preadolescence

Books for preadolescents often deal with the variety of problems these young-sters face. Since these books are concerned with the preadolescent's transition from childhood to young adulthood, they are often called coming of age books. During this period, preadolescents are torn between leaving the shelter of childhood and exploring the relationship of emerging adolescence. These are the years when a youngster may go to a school dance Friday evening and play with dolls Saturday afternoon.

Many young adult books deal with preadolescents' emerging independence and rapidly changing bodies. The best of these books help preadolescents deal with the confusion they feel. They present characters who still enjoy the games of child-hood, who ask questions about their changing bodies, who are in conflict with par-ents and teachers, who are unsure of their friends, and who learn to deal with these problems—often with the help of caring adults. Judy Blume is well known for her books dealing with preadolescence. *Are You There, God? It's Me, Margaret* is the story of a girl who is faced with her rapidly developing body, moving to a new town, mak-ing friends, and her parents' different religions. The protagonist in Blume's *Then Again, Maybe I Won't* deals with similar problems from the preteenage male perspec-tive. (An annotated bibliography of preadolescent coming of age books appears in Chapter 6.)

Many preadolescents' concerns and interests are like those they experienced as children. They still are interested in friendships with the same sex, slumber parties, games, animals, sports, daring adventures, camp, school, being part of the family, and having fun. Consequently, many books for this stage reflect these interests and concerns.

Early Adolescence

Early adolescence is often a lonely and frustrating time for young adults at-tempting to establish a personal identity as well as a place with their peers. Often adolescents feel isolated, as if no one else has ever faced the conflicts they are experi-encing. Young adult books can help them feel less alone while helping them develop mature reading interests.

Most young adult books deal with this difficult period in life. Characters in these books tend to be approximately the same age and experience problems similar to those of the readers.

Authors of young adult books become anonymous mentors who are able to speak to early adolescents as no adult on the scene can. They do this by talking through their young characters, not by talking down to readers. The best young adult books are written from the perspective of a young protagonist who is on eye level with readers.

It is only in adulthood that we can reflect on our own adolescence and under-stand it. Author Jerry Spinelli can talk to adolescents on eye level, in a way that parents, teachers, and most other adults in a young person's life cannot. He does it through the voices and actions of his young characters. Should he forget who he is as he writes and become Jerry Spinelli, father and adult author, young readers would immediately recognize the change. But this is not likely because Spinelli knows his readers and his characters too well; he remembers his own adolescence. He talks about his adolescence from his adult writer's perspective: "Like an old Brenda Lee 45, we spin on our backs for five seconds—looking back, that's all it seems, doesn't it—and then—poof!—we're grown up. But it was a glorious five seconds while it lasted—glorious and funny and excruciating and fascinating and significant. Worth remembering. Worth paying attention to. Worth writing about. Worth reading about."

In the best young adult books, the characters are anything but boring. They are young adults experiencing adolescence, and adolescence is rarely boring. Good young adult literature is honest; its characters are real people. Spinelli talks about creating such characters: "Does the writer wish to know people? Simple. Start with a single kid. Pick one out. Any one. Get to know him. All his colors and shading, all his moments. Because each kid is a population unto himself, a walking cross-section, a demographic grab bag, a child's bedroom is as much a window to the universe as a scientist's lab or a philosopher's study." Spinelli's characters speak to readers through the pages of the book. At the same time, Spinelli—the third person, anonymous adult—is speaking.

When they read young adult literature, early adolescents can share their problems with other young people, the characters in the book. Characters help adolescents examine their own problems with increased objectivity, stepping back, seeing them from a different perspective. And, since the protagonist has the mature perspective of the author, problems are likely to be viewed broadly in relation to all life has in store. Jesse, the 10 year old protagonist in Katherine Paterson's *Bridge to Terabithia*, reflects on the death of his best friend, Leslie.

> Now it was time for him to move out. She wasn't there, so he must go for both of them. It was up to him to pay back to the world in beauty and caring what Leslie had loaned him in vision and strength.
> As for the terrors ahead—for he did not fool himself that they were all behind him—well, you just have to stand up to your fear and not let it squeeze you white. Right, Leslie?

These are mature thoughts for a 10 year old, but Jesse is not just any 10 year old; he is a very real character in a book. Though most 10 year olds are unlikely to think the thoughts of Jesse, the hundreds of adolescents with whom I have discussed the book believe that the words are Jesse's and that they, like Jesse, can "see beyond to the shining world—huge and terrible and beautiful and very fragile. . . ."

Late Adolescence

In late adolescence teens begin to incorporate themselves into the adult community. During this period, young adults must make decisions that affect the rest of their lives. Too often they fail to consider the possible consequences of their actions and then find themselves in adult situations that force them to assume adult roles. A young man and woman who have not questioned their love may find themselves parents of an unwanted infant. A teenager who quits school may be unable to find employment.

Skilled authors are able to place late adolescent characters in situations common to adolescents and help readers discover the questions they must ask when faced with similar problems. Often the characters do not select the answers that are best for them and must suffer the consequences of their decisions.

Robert Lipsyte, a sports commentator and author of young adult books, claims that today's young people know the right answers but they don't know the right questions. He attempts to provide late adolescents with these questions.

Young adults' questions have no easy answers; often the "right" answers produce negative consequences. For example, in Robert Cormier's *The Chocolate War*, Jerry decides to oppose the powerful gang that rules his school. Readers never doubt the "rightness" of Jerry's decision. But Jerry suffers consequences; he is beaten by a member of the gang, and most of the adults in his life do not support his decision. The road of the righteous is often difficult. Cormier provides no answers, but the questions are clear to the reader.

As parents, most of us would like to shield our teenagers from situations in which they must ask these difficult questions. But in the real world people must learn to face difficult situations, ask appropriate questions, seek answers, and accept consequences. Teenagers who are unable to accomplish these tasks are not likely to become successful adults. Adolescents can share their problems with the characters in young adult books and discover that they are not alone.

Reading Young Adult Books Can Help Parents

Parents can read books written for young adults to learn to better understand their adolescents. Every year I teach a course in adolescent literature to adults, and there are always several students who are parents of adolescents. This is what one of them wrote to me at the end of the course.

> The books you asked us to read opened my eyes not only to wonderful books by wonderful writers, but to my 15-year-old son. Why didn't I remember my own adolescence? Why did it take me reading about someone else's to help me understand Rick? I don't know the answers. But, whatever they are, I am so thankful to have discovered these books. Rick and I are now reading *Killing Mr. Griffin* together. Discussing it with him is a real eye-opener. Now, if I could only convince his father to read them!

For many of us, the doors of conversation with our adolescents have been closed. Reading and sharing adolescent books can increase understanding and open doors to meaningful discussion. Young adult literature has the potential to guide our teenagers as they strive to meet the needs of social affection and self-esteem and to help us as we strive to understand them.

By sharing problems with characters in their books, teenage readers discover that their own problems are not unique.

Types of Young Adult Books

The world of young adult literature is rich. It includes all types of literature. According to author Richard Peck, the world of the adolescent is reflected in young adult books, with characters who are able to deal with the world using the wisdom of the books' adult authors. Similarly, because the authors of young adult books understand that their readers' lives are just beginning, the books usually end on a positive note that prepares "both protagonist and reader for a lot of life yet to be lived. The events [in the book] are a few experiences that nudge him or thrust him toward maturity."

What makes adolescent literature special is authors' ability to develop simple plots that become vehicles for the development of characters and their relationships. The best of these books make important points without preaching or talking down to their readers. They also create settings that transport egocentric adolescents to new worlds and allow readers to see these worlds through the eyes of realistic protagonists who possess insight and maturity beyond their years.

Coming of Age

Many young adult books deal with the developing adolescent and problems caused by the transition from childhood to adulthood. Characters in coming of age books usually progress through a series of events to reach more mature understanding. Literature can help egocentric adolescents to see beyond the moment and to understand the consequences of their actions. At the same time, these books can make adolescent readers feel less alone.

Historical Fiction

Though historical novels for young adults have been published for many years, they are gaining new popularity. This may be because the authors are increasingly aware of the needs and interests of their young readers. An increasing number of writers of young adult historical fiction are concerned with the historic accuracy of the work. Authors Christopher Collier and James Lincoln Collier provide a good example of recent trends in historical fiction for young adults. Their protagonists are young; they appear in accurate historic settings and face problems they would have faced in those settings, but they deal with these problems in ways today's young adults can understand.

Mystery and Suspense

Adolescents have always been attracted to mystery and suspense tales. In the past, about the only books available in this genre were serial books written by name-less authors hired to flesh out a plot outline prepared by a book syndicate, resulting in series such as Nancy Drew, the Hardy Boys, and Tom Swift. The books in these series had consistently good stories and predictable characters, but limited literary quality. Unfortunately, although young readers may have loved Nancy Drew or the Hardy Boys, they soon tired of the books' predictability. Until recently, these readers had to move directly from Nancy Drew to mysteries by adult authors such as Agatha Christie. For some readers this was not a problem, but those who were not ready for adult works often gave up reading entirely. Today, many fine suspense and mystery tales are published for adolescents.

Fantasy

There was a time when fantasy was considered inappropriate for anyone other than young children. This is no longer the case. J.R.R. Tolkien's *The Hobbit* and Ring Trilogy are popular with adults and adolescents and have an almost cult following. However, for many years there was nothing similar in the young adult marketplace. When author Madeleine L'Engle wrote *A Wrinkle in Time* in the 1960s, fantasy was established as an acceptable genre for young adult readers.

Like all young adult books, fantasies have young characters who deal with the problems of young readers. Since the major literary technique of the fantasy plot is a quest for good and for truth, there is probably no genre more appropriate to meet the needs of adolescents. What is adolescence if it is not a quest to discover who you are and where you fit into the world? Through fantasy literature, adolescents can find unexpected answers to their quest.

Science Fiction

Science fiction, like fantasy, allows readers to leave their limited universe and enter a world of limitless possibilities. The characters are realistic, but the obstacles they surmount are beyond the scope of the adolescent. The solutions they pursue often help real teenagers deal with everyday problems. Science fiction differs from fantasy in that the world is described according to the natural laws of science. Usually, the world is in an advanced scientific state; the fantastic things that happen are possible given what we know about science. Adolescents who are interested in science are often avid readers of science fiction. Likewise, readers of science fiction often develop an interest in the science on which the fiction is based.

Nonfiction

Nonfiction is an important part of the literature written for young adults. It shares many of the characteristics and attributes of young adult fiction. High quality nonfiction for adolescents has been available for only about twenty years. Prior to that time there was some nonfiction for children, but adolescents were expected to read material written for adults. According to W.G. Ellis, many adolescents today borrow nonfiction books more frequently than fiction from libraries.

Authors and publishers recognize the popularity of nonfiction on many topics. They also are aware that most adolescents are not yet ready for highly sophisticated adult works in the social sciences, arts, humanities, and sciences. The problems addressed in adult nonfiction are not the problems of most adolescents. Adolescents need their own nonfiction books that are stimulating and challenging and that address problems and issues from their perspectives.

The best nonfiction for adolescents is written by authorities in the fields in which they write. Many writers are known for both their adult writings and their young adult books. Most recognize the importance of introducing teenagers to issues, questions, ideas, concepts, and skills in terms they can understand. Good young adult nonfiction differs from adult nonfiction in terms of complexity, not in terms of quality of content or writing.

Young adult nonfiction is not condensed from adult books. On the few occasions when adult nonfiction has been reissued for adolescents, it has been rewritten by knowledgeable writers, not simply condensed. Good young adult nonfiction is characterized by accuracy, good writing, appropriate illustrations, authoritative writing, good bibliographies of appropriate sources, and appropriate placement of visuals within the text. (Many fine works of nonfiction for young adults are discussed in Chapter 7.)

Poetry

Poetry collections for young adults are a rather recent phenomenon. For many years, there were few anthologies of poems appropriate for adolescents. The poems adolescents read generally appeared in school literature anthologies and were written by adult authors for adult readers. Today, a variety of poetry books are published for adolescents.

Probably the most popular type of poetry is the anthology of poems on a single theme or topic. Often these anthologies include works written by adults for adults, but these poems are selected with the interests and needs of adolescents in mind.

Similarly, anthologists have begun collecting the works of a single poet and editing them so they are appropriate for adolescents. This has made the poetry of Carl Sandburg, Emily Dickinson, Sylvia Plath, and many others accessible and interesting to young adults.

Collections of poems written specifically for adolescents also are available. Shel Silverstein is the acknowledged master of this technique for preadolescent readers. Poets such as Nancy Willard, Eve Merriam, and Lilian Moore have gained recognition for their young adult work.

In addition, anthologists have been collecting work written by young adult poets. This work has been published in anthologies dealing with specific themes or issues. (Many anthologies and poetry collections are listed in Chapter 7.)

Conclusion

Young adult books are written for all the developmental stages of the adolescent, and every type of literature present in the adult marketplace is available to adolescent readers. The best of these books speak to adolescents from the perspective of adolescent characters, but deal with the problems of adolescence with greater maturity than most adolescents possess.

Parents who are aware of the books of young adulthood often can provide the right book at the right time. Likewise, parents who read these books are likely to gain new perspectives on their teenagers' problems and concerns.

Chapter 6

Fiction Kids Love

Several thousand books for young adults are published each year, making the selection of appropriate books for preadolescent and adolescent readers challenging.

The following annotated bibliography lists books appropriate for readers from ages 10 through 18. It is divided into two sections: fiction (Chapter 6) and nonfiction (Chapter 7). Each category has numerous subcategories to help you select books based on the adolescent's interests.

An indication of the general age range for which the book is appropriate is provided in each entry. This age range should guide you in selecting or suggesting books.

PA   Preadolescent (ages 10-13)
EA   Early Adolescent (ages 13-15)
LA   Late Adolescent (ages 15-18)

The publisher of each book and the year of publication are listed after the title and author. If the book is available in paperback, the publisher of that edition is listed with the word "paper." Other information includes whether males (**M**) or females (**F**) are more likely to enjoy the book, a star (*) if books are appropriate for poor readers, and a plus (+) if books are especially good for reading aloud.

Animals

The Bear, William Faulkner. In **Three Famous Short Novels.** Random House, paper, 1958.

A classic hunting story about a search for a legendary bear combined with an exploration of corruption versus innocence. **LA**

The Black Stallion, Walter Farley. Random House, paper, 1944.

The heartwarming story of a boy, a horse, a shipwreck, and a race. Other books in the series include **Son of the Black Stallion, The Black Stallion and Satan,** and **The Island Stallion. PA * +**

The Cry of the Crow, Jean Craighead George. Harper & Row, paper, 1980.

The author, who is intimately familiar with animals, tells a wonderful story about a girl and a crow that mimics hunters. **PA EA +**

Hawkmistress!, Marion Zimmer Bradley. New American Library, paper, 1982.

Romilly MacAran's father forbids her to use her gift of communication with animals and forces her to marry a man she does not love. She escapes to the hills of Darkover to flee her fate. **EA LA F**

The Incredible Journey, A Tale of Three Animals, Sheila Burnford. Little, Brown, 1961. Bantam, paper.

Tells the story of two dogs and a cat on a long homeward trek. **EA +**

Julie of the Wolves, Jean Craighead George. Harper & Row, paper, 1972.

A Newbery Award winning book about a young girl's struggle to survive on the North Slope of Alaska with the help of a pack of Arctic wolves. **PA EA F * +**

King of the Wind, Marguerite Henry. Macmillan, paper, 1948.

Tells of a mute boy's love for a championship horse. **PA +**

Summer of the Monkeys, Wilson Rawls. Doubleday, 1977. Dell, paper.

Jay Berry takes on the task of capturing a tribe of escaped monkeys in the Oklahoma mountains. **PA**

A Time to Fly Free, Stephanie S. Tolan. Scribner, 1983.

A bright but belligerent boy leaves school to work for a man who cares for injured birds. He learns many things from the experience. **PA**

Watership Down, Richard Adams. Macmillan, 1974. Avon, paper.

A fantasy about the breakup of a rabbit warren and the rabbits' search for a new home. Though parts can be shared with the entire family, its length makes it more appropriate for older readers. (Appropriate for reading aloud **PA EA LA .) LA +**

Where the Red Fern Grows, Wilson Rawls. Doubleday, 1974.

During the Depression, Billy buys and trains two coon dogs. He wins a gold cup in the annual coon contest and learns about love and trust. **PA * +**

Black Heroes

The Autobiography of Miss Jane Pitman, Ernest Gaines. Doubleday, 1971.
Bantam, paper.
This fictional account of Jane Pitman, who was born a slave and freed soon
after the Civil War, takes readers from the Civil War to the 1960s. The story
begins with Jane as an adolescent and describes the years of her marriage and
her old age when she witnesses and participates in the civil rights
movement.   **EA LA** +

Freedom Road, Howard Fast. Bantam, paper, 1970.
This historic novel set in the South of Reconstruction is about a former slave
who dreams of beginning a community where blacks and whites can live
together. Based on facts and events of this period.   **EA LA**

The Friends, Rosa Guy. Holt, Rinehart & Winston, 1973. Bantam, paper.
A lonely girl in Harlem learns that appearance is not as important as
friendship. In the sequel, **Edith Jackson** (Viking), Edith tries to keep her
family together after the death of her parents.   **EA F** *

A Gathering of Old Men, Ernest Gaines. Knopf, 1983. Random House, paper.
After a white man feared by blacks is killed, a white woman and a dozen old
black men claim to have killed him. They are all protecting someone
important to them.   **LA**

A Hero Ain't Nothin' but a Sandwich, Alice Childress. Coward, McCann, &
Geoghegan, 1973. Avon, paper.
This story of a 13 year old drug user is told from his own perspective as well as
those of his mother, grandmother, stepfather, teachers, and friends.   **EA LA** *

If Beale Street Could Talk, James Baldwin. Dial, 1974. New American Library,
paper.
In this masterful book a young man is framed and jailed while he and his
girlfriend are supported by a loyal family.   **LA**

Invisible Man, Ralph Ellison. Random House, 1951. Modern Library, paper.
A nameless hero learns that his search for identity involves confrontation
with whites and blacks. A classic story of innocence and answers.   **LA**

Ludell's New York Time, Brenda Wilkinson. Harper & Row, 1980.
In this sequel to **Ludell and Willie** (Harper & Row, 1977, Bantam, paper. *)
and **Ludell** (Harper & Row, 1975, Bantam, paper. *), Ludell has left her rural
Georgia home after her grandmother's death. She finds that New York offers
nothing but dead end jobs and wants to go home to marry Willie.   **EA LA F** *

M.C. Higgins, the Great, Virginia Hamilton. Macmillan, 1974. Dell, paper.
A lyrical story about a boy whose only special talent is sitting atop a flag pole.
He learns that life is far more than sitting and watching the world go by.
Readers who enjoy this book also are likely to enjoy **A Little Love**
(Philomel, 1984, Berkley, paper) and **A White Romance** (Philomel, 1987).
EA LA

Mojo and the Russian, Walter Dean Myers. Viking, 1977.
Dean believes Drusilla has placed a voodoo spell on him, and his gang devises a plan to "unfix" him from the spell. In the process they meet the "Russian spy." **The Young Landlords** (Viking, 1979, * +) is another book with the same humorous characters.   **PA EA M * +**

The Original Colored House of David, Martin Quigley. Houghton Mifflin, 1981.
In the midwest in the late 1920s, Timmy seeks a chance to prove his manliness and athletic skill.   **EA M**

Rainbow Jordan, Alice Childress. Coward, McCann, & Geoghegan, 1981. Avon, paper.
A moving story about three black women. Rainbow, 14, is frequently left alone by her mother. Because of her mother's neglect, she meets Miss Josephine, a loving older woman sent by Social Services when Rainbow is left alone for several days.   **EA F**

Roll of Thunder Hear My Cry, Mildred Taylor. Dial, 1976. Bantam, paper.
The story of a black family's struggle to maintain dignity and self-respect in the poverty of the 1930s in Mississippi. This book and its sequel, **Let the Circle Be Unbroken** (Dial, 1981, Bantam, paper. +), contrast family love with the prejudice that pervades the community.   **EA LA +**

This Strange New Feeling, Julius Lester. Dial, 1982. Scholastic, paper.
Three stories tied together by a common plot in which black Americans attempt to gain freedom during the antebellum period.   **EA LA**

To Kill a Mockingbird, Harper Lee. Harper & Row, 1961. Warner, paper.
Describes life in a small Alabama town through the eyes of a young girl who observes her father's courtroom defense of a black man accused of raping a white woman.   **EA LA +**

Words by Heart, Ouida Sebestyen. Little, Brown, 1979. Bantam, paper.
In the early 1900s, prejudice against blacks in the West makes it difficult for Lena Sills to find a home. Through her family's love she finds a place for herself.   **EA F * +**

Coming of Age

Anywhere Else but Here, Bruce Clement. Farrar, Straus & Giroux, 1980. Dell, paper.
Molly wants to begin a new life anywhere else but here. Through determination she succeeds despite people who attempt to get in the way of her dream.   **EA LA F**

Behave Yourself, Bethany Brant, Patricia Beatty. Morrow, 1986.
>Bethany, the daughter of a circuit preacher in turn of the century Texas, tries to do the right thing, but finds it difficult to be good. The book never preaches, but leads readers to self-awareness by Bethany's example.
>PA EA F *

Bridges to Cross, Paul Janeczko. Macmillan, 1986.
>James is trying to establish his own identity when his mother forces him to attend a strict parochial school. Finally, his mother comes to terms with her son's need to establish a personal ethic.   EA M

Bridge to Terabithia, Katherine Paterson. Crowell, 1979. Avon, paper.
>A Newbery Award book about a 10 year old who dreams of being the fastest runner in the fifth grade, but learns that friendship is more important.
>PA EA +

The Catcher in the Rye, J.D. Salinger. Little, Brown, 1951. Bantam, paper.
>In this classic coming of age novel, Holden leaves his prep school in Pennsylvania and goes underground in New York City for three days while he tries to sort out his life.   LA

Cat Herself, Mollie Hunter. Harper & Row, 1986.
>This book about Cat, who sets out to establish herself at a time when women were not expected to be heard, could be classified historical fiction.   EA F

Come Sing, Jimmy Jo, Katherine Paterson. Lodestar, 1985.
>James joins his family's country music singing group, but doesn't want to be different from the other kids at school.   PA EA *

Dark but Full of Diamonds, Katie Letcher Lyle. Coward, McCann, & Geoghegan, 1981.
>Scott, 16, is hopelessly in love with his English and drama teacher. When his father and the teacher announce that they plan to be married, Scott gets drunk and treats the people around him badly. His actions make Hilah and his father give up their marriage plans, but Scott experiences no victory.
>EA LA

A Day No Pigs Would Die, Robert Newton Peck. Knopf, 1972. Dell, paper.
>A story of life and death on a Vermont farm. Because of the simplicity of the plot and the complexity of the theme, this book can be read and enjoyed by readers of all ages.   EA +

Downtown, Norma Fox Mazer. Morrow, 1984. Avon, paper.
>Pete's parents leave him with his uncle when they flee to avoid prosecution for a crime. Pete must try to find his own identity without telling anyone who he really is.   EA LA *

Edisto, Padgett Powell. Farrar, Straus & Giroux, 1984. Holt, Rinehart & Winston, paper.
>Simons, 12, attempts to make sense of the black-white world in which he has grown up. This book is for only the most sophisticated adolescent readers.
>LA

Enoch's Place, Joyce Rockwood. Holt, Rinehart & Winston, 1980.
> Enoch is raised in an isolated, rural community. Despite his warm feelings about his home, he moves to the city, but finds it to be superficial and unfriendly. He returns home with his values reaffirmed. **EA**

Far from Shore, Kevin Major. Delacorte, 1981. Dell, paper.
> Chris, 16, blames his small town and his home for his problems. The story, told from the shifting perspectives of Chris and his friends and family, is about Chris' misbehavior and his slow acceptance of responsibility for his own actions. **EA LA M**

Gentlehands, M.E. Kerr. Harper & Row, 1978. Bantam, paper.
> Buddy's world seems to collapse when he falls in love and then discovers that his grandfather is a Nazi war criminal. **EA ***

The Girl, Robbie Branscum. Harper & Row, 1986.
> This autobiographical novel portrays the struggles of growing up in the poverty of the Arkansas hills. It realistically portrays sexual abuse and sibling courage. Though the book is written for early adolescents, parents may want to read and discuss it with their children. **PA EA F**

The Giver, Lynn Hall. Scribner, 1985.
> A 15 year old girl and her teacher are attracted to one another. Through his honesty and concern, both grow in confidence and courage. **EA F**

The Green of Me, Patricia Lee Gauch. Putnam, 1978.
> As 17 year old Jennifer is traveling on a train to visit her boyfriend, Chris, she reflects on her childhood and her relationship with Chris. **EA LA F**

Harry & Hortense at Hormone High, Paul Zindel. Harper & Row, 1984. Bantam, paper.
> Harry and Hortense learn about hero workship from Jason, a schizophrenic who believes he is the reincarnation of Icarus. When Jason commits suicide, Harry and Hortense learn about the hero within each of them. **LA**

The Horse Trader, Lynn Hall. Scribner, 1981.
> On one level, this is the story of 15 year old Karen who worships horse trainer Harley Williams. On another level, it deals with Karen's growth as she discovers the truth about Harley, her illegitimacy, and her relationship with her mother. **EA F**

A House Like a Lotus, Madeleine L'Engle. Farrar, Straus & Giroux, 1984. Dell, paper.
> As Polly, 17, travels through Greece, her reflections on the events of the previous school year allow her to find her own path to understanding and love. **EA LA F**

In Summer Light, Zibby Oneal. Viking, 1985. Bantam, paper.
> Kate learns to accept her own abilities and strengths as separate from her exceptionally talented artist father. **EA LA F**

Is That You, Miss Blue?, M.E. Kerr. Harper & Row, 1975. Dell, paper.
> Flanders is sent to boarding school and learns about cruelty, friendship, and caring. **PA EA F * +**

Jacob Have I Loved, Katherine Paterson. Crowell, 1980. Avon, paper.
In this Newbery Award book, Louise searches for her own identity while fighting jealousy of her talented, beautiful, and fragile twin.   **EA F**

The Language of Goldfish, Zibby Oneal. Viking, 1980. Fawcett, paper.
Because she is afraid of growing up, Carrie suffers a mental breakdown and retreats to the safety of childhood.   **EA LA F**

The Leaving, Lynn Hall. Scribner, 1980. Ace, paper.
Roxanne graduates from high school and decides that a job in the city is the ticket to happiness.   **EA LA F**

Midnight Hour Encores, Bruce Brooks. Harper & Row, paper, 1986.
Sibilance, a 16 year old who has been raised by her father, sets out to find her mother and discovers the importance of her father's love and support.   **EA**

The Moves Make the Man, Bruce Brooks. Harper & Row, paper, 1984.
Jerome is the first black student in a high school in the 1950s. The novel tells about his friendship with a troubled young man struggling with his mother's mental illness and his stepfather's antagonism.   **EA LA ***

My Antonia, Willa Cather. Houghton Mifflin, paper, 1918.
Antonia, a daughter of immigrants, finds a place for herself on the land and in the community.   **LA F**

Notes for Another Life, Sue Ellen Bridgers. Knopf, 1981.
Kevin and Wren must discover their identities while living with their grandparents and struggling to understand their father's mental illness and their mother's desire to live away from her children.   **EA LA +**

One-Eyed Cat, Paula Fox. Bradbury, 1984. Dell, paper.
Ned must deal with his guilt after injuring a cat with an air rifle. Eventually he learns to understand what he has done.   **EA LA**

Over the Moon, Elissa Haden Guest. Morrow, 1986.
Kate has lived with her aunt since her parents died. When she goes to visit her older sister, she comes to terms with her own identity.   **EA LA F**

Permanent Connections, Sue Ellen Bridgers. Harper & Row, 1987.
Sixteen year old Bob is forced to care for his aunt and grandfather in their Appalachian mountain home. He finds his own identity in the rugged mountains.   **EA LA**

A Portrait of the Artist as a Young Man, James Joyce. Penguin, paper, 1916.
This stream of consciousness monologue takes Stephen from childhood to early manhood. For very mature adolescent readers.   **LA**

Prank, Kathryn Lasky. Macmillan, 1984. Dell, paper.
Birdie finds a metaphor for her life in the chipped madonna that stands among the weeds in her front yard.   **LA**

A Separate Peace, John Knowles. Macmillan, 1960. Dell, paper.
An unspoken rivalry between two friends in a New England prep school mirrors the beginning of World War II. **Peace Breaks Out** (Bantam, paper, 1982) is its long awaited sequel.   **EA LA**

A Solitary Blue, Cynthia Voigt. Macmillan, 1983. Fawcett, paper.
> Jeff thinks the solitary blue heron is a good symbol for his life until he learns the importance of his father's love. **EA M +**

Summer of My German Soldier, Bette Greene. Dial, 1973. Bantam, paper.
> A Jewish girl feels all alone in her Arkansas town during World War II until she befriends a German prisoner of war. In its sequel, **Morning Is a Long Time Coming** (Dial, 1979, Archway, paper), Patty searches for the prisoner's parents to tell them of his death. **EA LA F * +**

Thirty-Six Exposures, Kevin Major. Delacorte, 1984.
> Lorne searches for himself through photographs he takes to complete a class project. **EA LA M**

Three Sisters, Norma Fox Mazer. Scholastic, 1986.
> Karen feels overshadowed by her older sisters and nearly destroys her relationship with her family. **EA F**

Tiger Eyes, Judy Blume. Bradbury, 1981. Dell, paper.
> After her father's murder, Davey meets Wolf, whose father is dying of cancer. **EA LA F ***

Travelers, Larry Bograd. Lippincott, 1986.
> Jack has built a superman image of his father, who was killed in Vietnam. In learning the truth about his father, he learns much about himself. **EA LA M**

Underneath I'm Different, Ellen Rabinowich. Delacorte, 1983. Dell, paper.
> An overweight girl learns to overcome her problems when she meets a fellow student with serious psychological problems. He helps convince her of her own worth and enables her to move out from under her mother's overprotection. **EA F ***

Where the Lilies Bloom, Vera Cleaver and Bill Cleaver. Lippincott, 1969. New American Library, paper.
> Several children are left on their own in the mountains after their father dies. They survive by wild-crafting, collecting plants for medicinal purposes. **Trial Valley** (Lippincott, 1987, * +) is the sequel. **PA EA * +**

Yesterday's Daughter, Patricia Calvert. Scribner, 1986.
> An illegitimate girl meets a photographer whose photographs teach her to look at her life from a different angle. **EA F**

Death

About David, Susan Beth Pheffer. Delacorte, 1980. Dell, paper.
> David murders his adoptive parents and kills himself. Lynn, his friend since childhood, must find out why before she can confront her feelings about him. **EA LA ***

Close Enough to Touch, Richard Peck. Delacorte, 1981. Dell, paper.
Matt has barely recovered from his mother's death when his girlfriend dies. Though his father and stepmother are loving and supportive, they are unable to understand the depth of his grief. It is not until he meets Margaret that he is able to come to terms with death and life. **EA LA ***

A Formal Feeling, Zibby Oneal. Viking, 1982. Fawcett, paper.
Anne is obsessed by the memory of her dead mother. Her obsession, which is more awe of her mother's many talents than love, haunts the rest of Anne's family. **EA LA F**

Friends till the End, Todd Strasser. Delacorte, 1981. Dell, paper.
Howie, who is suffering from leukemia, is a new student at David's high school. Through their friendship, David comes to terms with the priorities in his life. **EA ***

A Ring of Endless Light, Madeleine L'Engle. Farrar, Straus & Giroux, 1980. Dell, paper.
This book is more about life than about death. Vicky struggles with her grandfather's slow death as she learns about life while working with dolphins. **EA F * +**

The Summer Before, Patricia Windsor. Harper & Row, 1973. Dell, paper.
Alexandra must come to terms with her best friend's death. Her parents, a friend, and her psychiatrist help her deal with "losing the first person you ever loved." **EA F**

Sunshine, Norma Klein. Avon, paper, 1974.
Kate has bone cancer, but refuses treatment because it might distort her life. The book is in the form of a tape recorded diary from Kate for her daughter. **EA LA F ***

A Taste of Blackberries, Doris Buchanan Smith. Crowell, 1973. Scholastic, paper.
Jamie's best friend is stung by a bee and dies. Jamie blames himself for not doing something to prevent it. At the funeral, Jamie begins to deal with the tragedy and death. **PA EA +**

Waiting for Johnny Miracle, Alice Bach. Harper & Row, 1980. Bantam, paper.
One twin sister discovers she has bone cancer; the other is healthy. The novel deals with their attempts to come to terms with this difference and with the emotional impact on the family, life in the pediatric cancer ward, and their struggle to keep life as normal as possible. **EA LA**

When the Phone Rang, Harry Mazer. Scholastic, paper, 1985.
The phone call told the Keller children that their parents had been killed in a plane crash. The story is about how the three teenage children deal with this tragic loss. **EA ***

Ethnic Heroes

Chernowitz!, Fran Arrick. Bradbury, 1981. New American Library, paper.
Cherno tries to ignore the anti-Semitic remarks of the class bully. Action by his parents and the principal brings the prejudice into the open. **EA**

Child of the Owl, Laurence Yep. Harper & Row, 1977.
Casey, a Chinese-American girl, has lived a nomadic life with her gambler father. When her father is hospitalized and she is sent to stay with her grandmother, she begins to search for her identity. **EA +**

The Chosen, Chaim Potok. Simon & Schuster, 1967. Fawcett, paper.
A young Hasidic Jew searches for his identity in New York City. Another Potok book on a similar topic is **My Name Is Asher Lev** (Knopf, 1972, Fawcett, paper). **LA**

Davita's Harp, Chaim Potok. Knopf, 1985. Fawcett, paper.
Davita lives with her politically involved parents in New York City in the 1930s and 1940s. Her parents have defied their religious heritage, and she must search for hers. **LA F**

Eyes of Darkness, Jamake Highwater. Lothrop, Lee & Shepard, 1985.
This book, based on the true story of a Santee Indian physician at the time of the Wounded Knee massacre, is the story of a sensitive young man who has dedicated himself to bringing two cultures together. **EA LA +**

Ganesh, Malcolm J. Bosse. Crowell, 1981.
Ganesh moves to the rural American Midwest when his father dies in India. At first he is isolated from other young people who consider his knowledge of yoga and Indian philosophies strange. **EA**

I Wear the Morning Star, Jamake Highwater. Harper & Row, 1986.
This third book in the Ghost Horse Cycle is the story of Sitko, a young First American who searches for his identity. Sitko is an artist who paints the stories told to him by his grandmother. The other two books in the cycle are **Legend Days** (Harper & Row, 1984 +) and **The Ceremony of Innocence** (Harper & Row, 1985 +). **PA EA LA +**

Mountain Light, Laurence Yep. Harper & Row, 1985.
The setting for this novel is the 1855 rebellion in China. Squeaky thinks he is a coward and becomes a clown, a trait that serves him well against his enemies. When he flees China he discovers the feuds still exist in America. **PA EA +**

When the Legends Die, Hal Borland. Lippincott, 1963. Bantam, paper.
Thomas punishes the rodeo horse he rides until a terrible accident sends him back to the mountains of his Indian youth. **EA**

Fantasy

Animal Farm, George Orwell. Harcourt Brace Jovanovich, 1954. New American Library, paper.
    This fantasy/satire is the tale of rebellious animals who attempt to create a society based on equality. **LA**

The Beginning Place, Ursala LeGuin. Harper & Row, 1980.
    Two alienated teenagers discover the fantasy world of Tembreabrezi while trying to escape from the real world. There they confront their personal problems, fears, and frustrations. **LA**

Dragon's Blood, Jane Yolen. Delacorte, 1982. Dell, paper.
    Jakkin's tale of dragon stealing, training, and fighting is aided by a young girl who becomes his first love. The sequels, **Heart's Blood** (Delacorte, 1986, Dell, paper * +) and **A Sending of Dragons** (Delacorte, 1987), tell us more of the adventures of Jakkin, who is now a young Dragon Master. **PA * +**

The Darkangel, Meredith Ann Pierce. Little, Brown, 1982. Warner, paper.
    The Darkangel is a vampire who kidnaps Eoduin to become his 13th bride. Aeriel seeks to free the wives, but is kidnapped herself. Aeriel's growing attachment for the vampire makes it difficult to achieve her goal of freeing the wives. **A Gathering of Gargoyles** (Little, 1984, Warner, paper) is the second book of the trilogy in which Aeriel travels to a strange land in search of the answer to a riddle. **EA LA**

Dragon of the Lost Sea, Laurence Yep. Harper & Row, 1982.
    This tale is based loosely on a Chinese myth about the efforts of the shape changing dragon Shimmer to restore her clan's traditional home. **PA EA**

The Flight of the Cassowary, John LeVert. Atlantic, 1986.
    John is metamorphosed into rats and horses after he begins talking to Ken, a neighborhood dog. In this fantasy, John does not totally leave his real world, and this causes problems for him. **EA LA**

The Hero and the Crown, Robin McKinley. Greenwillow, 1985. Berkley, paper.
    Aerin is a strong female heroine who takes on dragon killing when her father refuses to let her ride into battle with the warriors. The fact that she is a motherless misfit princess should appeal to many adolescent girls. Readers who enjoy this tale may also enjoy its prequel, **The Blue Sword** (Greenwillow, 1982, Berkley, paper). **EA F**

The Left Hand of Darkness, Ursula LeGuin. Harper & Row, 1976. Ace, paper.
    This book deals with a technologically primitive world in which Ali must face a hostile climate, a contentious government, and his own sexuality. **EA**

The Legend of Tarik, Walter Dean Myers. Viking, 1981. Scholastic, paper.
    This unusual story is about a black teenage hero who is avenging his family's slaughter. **EA**

The Lion, the Witch, and the Wardrobe, C.S. Lewis. Macmillan, paper, 1986.
    This classic fantasy, composed as a Christian metaphor, catalogs four children's adventures in the land of Narnia. **PA +**

The Lord of the Rings, J.R.R. Tolkien. Allen, 1954.

> This epic fantasy trilogy written for adults is loved by many older adolescents. Middle Earth becomes the battleground between good and evil as Frodo struggles to destroy the ring and the evil it represents. **LA**

Moreta: Dragon Lady of Pern, Anne McCaffrey. Ballantine, paper, 1984.

> This book explores the planet of Pern (as do six earlier overlapping books in the Dragonriders of Pern series), a land in which dragons and their telepathic riders protect the world from deadly silver threads. The books have realistic, earthy characters. **EA F**

The Shadow Guests, Joan Aiken. Delacorte, 1980. Dell, paper.

> In this cross between fantasy and science fiction, Aiken explores Einstein's theory of relativity, parapsychology, and mysticism to allow Cosmo to encounter three of his ancestors just before they fall victim to a curse. **EA LA**

Westmark, Lloyd Alexander. Dutton, 1981. Dell, paper.

> In this first book of the Westmark Trilogy (**The Kestral,** Dutton, 1983, Dell, paper and **The Beggar Queen,** Dutton, 1984, Dell, paper), Theo is forced to leave town because of a murder he thinks he committed. He becomes involved with a medicine showman, a dwarf, a beautiful girl, and Cabbarus, who is influencing the King against him. **PA +**

A Wrinkle in Time, Madeleine L'Engle. Farrar, Straus & Giroux, 1962. Dell, paper.

> This is the first of L'Engle's Time Trilogy (**A Swiftly Tilting Planet,** Farrar, Straus & Giroux, 1978, Dell, paper and **A Wind in the Door,** Farrar, Straus & Giroux, 1973, Dell, paper). Three young people transcend time to rescue their father. All three books are filled with science, the supernatural, and religion. **PA EA +**

Folklore, Legend, Myth, and Religion

The Beast, Jonathan Fast. Random House, 1981. Ballantine, paper.

> A contemporary version of the traditional tale of "Beauty and the Beast" in which Beauty is a movie actress and Beast is a former napalm chemical company director. **EA LA F +**

Beauty: A Retelling of the Story of Beauty and the Beast, Robin McKinley. Harper & Row, 1978. Pocket Books, paper.

> This is a traditional but much expanded retelling of the classic fairy tale. **PA EA LA F +**

Fair Day and Another Step Begun, Katie Letcher Lyle. Lippincott, 1974. Dell, paper.

> This contemporary novel is based on the "Childe Waters" English ballad. Ellen, pregnant by John, is determined to keep the child and marry John. He is equally determined to abandon her and the child. **EA LA F**

The Hunchback of Notre Dame, Victor Hugo, adapted by Diana Stewart.
    Raintree, 1981.
    This is one of the best of the retellings of this classic tale; illustrations are
    included. **EA**
The Magical Adventures of Pretty Pearl, Virginia Hamilton. Harper & Row,
    1983. Harper & Row, paper.
    Hamilton combines American and black legend and folklore to create a story
    of Pretty Pearl, god child from Mount Kenya who convinces her brother and
    best god to take her among the humans. After flying to America as an
    albatross, Pretty Pearl assumes the shape of a human child and begins her
    quest to help free blacks. **PA EA**
The Maid of the North and Other Folktale Heroines, Ethel Johnston Phelps.
    Holt, Rinehart & Winston, 1981.
    These twenty-one tales from many countries have ingenious, determined
    heroines. **EA LA F**
The Road to Camlann: The Death of King Arthur, Rosemary Sutcliff.
    Dutton, 1982.
    This is one of the best retellings of Arthurian legend for young adults. The
    other books in the trilogy are **The Sword and the Circle** (Dutton, 1981)
    and **The Light Beyond the Forest** (Dutton, 1980). **PA EA +**
Seven Daughters and Seven Sons, Barbara Cohen and Bahija Lovejoy.
    Macmillan, 1982.
    This is a retelling of a traditional Arabic tale in which a poor merchant's
    daughter, disguised as a boy, makes a fortune and takes revenge against seven
    male cousins. **PA EA F**
Siddhartha, Hermann Hesse. New Directions, 1951. Bantam, paper.
    This has been nearly a cult book for several generations of young adults.
    Siddhartha has a variety of experiences and pleasures until he ascends to a
    state of peace and mystic holiness. **LA**

Handicaps and Illness

Go Ask Alice, Anonymous. Prentice Hall, 1971. Avon, paper.
    This is one of the most popular of all adolescent books, as timely today as
    when it was written. It is a frank diary of a 15 year old girl's terrifying
    experiences with drugs. **EA LA**
I Never Promised You a Rose Garden, Joanne Greenberg. Holt, Rinehart &
    Winston, 1964. New American Library, paper.
    A popular book in which a young girl journeys back from madness to
    sanity. **EA**
Just One Friend, Lynn Hall. Scribner, 1985.
    Dory, age 16, has learning disabilities. She tries to stop her friend from riding
    in another girl's new car and inadvertently causes a fatal accident. **EA F ***

41

The Language of Goldfish, Zibby Oneal. Viking, 1980. Fawcett, paper.
>   Carrie, an upperclass teenager, is beginning to lose grip on reality. A suicide
>   attempt puts her in the hospital, where she gets the help she needs.   EA LA

Lisa, Bright and Dark, John Neufeld. New American Library, paper, 1970.
>   Lisa is an intelligent teenager on the brink of insanity, but her parents and
>   teachers refuse to acknowledge her problem. Only three friends can help Lisa
>   cope with her illness.   EA LA *

The People Therein, Mildred Lee. Houghton Mifflin, 1980.
>   A lame 18 year old Appalachian girl meets and falls in love with a botanist
>   from Boston.   LA F

Perdita, Isabelle Holland. Little, Brown 1983. Fawcett, paper.
>   Perdita is in an accident and develops amnesia. The author weaves a mystery
>   around the discovery of every new memory.   PA EA F *

Wheels for Walking, Sandra Richmond. Atlantic, 1983.
>   A ski weekend turns into tragedy for Sally when she severs her spinal cord in
>   a car accident. She must adjust to life as a quadraplegic. The ending is
>   optimistic.   EA LA F *

Winning, Robin Brancato. Knopf, 1977. Bantam, paper.
>   The story of a young man whose football injury results in permanent
>   paralysis. The story is told from the perspectives of the young man, his
>   girlfriend, and his English teacher. He learns that winning involves far more
>   than physical prowess.   EA LA * +

With You & Without You, Ann M. Martin. Holiday, 1986.
>   Liza and her siblings must deal with the knowledge of their father's heart
>   disease.   PA EA *

Historical Fiction

Across Five Aprils, Irene Hunt. Follett, 1964. Ace, paper.
>   Jethro is too young to fight in the Civil War, but he watches his older brothers
>   go off to opposing armies. His parents are stricken by grief and suffering as the
>   neighbors seek vengeance.   EA LA +

All Quiet on the Western Front, Erich M. Remarque. Little, Brown, 1929.
Fawcett, paper.
>   A young World War I German soldier experiences the horrors of war in this
>   classic novel.   LA M

Beyond the Divide, Kathryn Lasky. Macmillan, 1983. Dell, paper.
>   Fourteen year old Meribah accompanies her father on the '49 Gold Rush,
>   leaving her Pennsylvania Amish community. Hardships along the way,
>   including the rape of a friend and the deaths of that friend and her father,
>   lead to Meribah being taken in by the Yahi Indians.   PA LA +

Cave under the City, Harry Mazer. Crowell, 1986.
> During the Depression, Tolley experiences hardships when he must assume responsibility for his 5 year old brother. **EA ***

The Clan of the Cave Bear, Jean Auel. Crown, 1980. Bantam, paper.
> The first and best of Auel's prehistoric series is appropriate for young readers. A Cro-Magnon girl is adopted by a tribe of Neanderthals and struggles to subdue her abilities while growing up in a mystical and male dominated society. **LA F**

The Fighting Ground, Avi. Lippincott, 1985.
> In 1778, 13 year old Jonathan joins the American militia against his father's wishes. Instead of glory, he experiences pain, brutality, and death. **EA +**

Frontier Wolf, Rosemary Sutcliff. Dutton, 1981.
> In fourth century A.D. Britain, Centurion Alexios is disgraced and sent to an outpost on the Firth of Forth. His skill and courage redeem his reputation as a Roman commander. **EA +**

I Am Rosemarie, Marietta D. Moskin. Day, 1972. Dell, paper.
> In this autobiographical novel, the author catalogs the human triumphs of the Holocaust. Rosemarie spends her early teenage years hiding in a series of German settlement camps. She shares these years with her family and remains grateful and optimistic throughout. **PA EA LA F**

I Be Somebody, Hadley Irwin. Macmillan, 1984. New American Library, paper.
> Rap and other black citizens are hoodwinked into buying seats on the freedom train to Athabasca in Canada during this little known episode in black American history. **PA EA * +**

Johnny Tremain, Esther Forbes. Houghton Mifflin, 1943. Dell, paper.
> In this classic work, Johnny dreams of becoming a silversmith, but his dreams are dashed when his right hand is burned and crippled. As he seeks a new way of life he is led into the intrigue and adventure of the Boston Tea Party. **PA +**

Jump Ship to Freedom, James L. Collier and Christopher Collier. Delacorte, 1981. Dell, paper.
> This book deals with Daniel, the son of a slave, who was willed Continental notes to secure his freedom following the Revolution. **War Comes to Willie Freeman** (Delacorte, 1987, Dell, paper +) and **Who Is Carrie?** (Delacorte, 1984, Dell, paper +) are sequels. **PA +**

The Last Mission, Harry Mazer. Dell, paper.
> Loosely based on an incident in the author's own life, this book is about a teenager who enlists in the World War II United States Air Force using his brother's birth certificate as proof of age. He expects to find glory in war, but finds horror and hardship instead. **EA LA M ***

Leif the Unlucky, Erik Christian Haugaard. Houghton Mifflin, 1982.
> Leif attempts to save his 15th century Norse settlement from extinction. **PA**

The Massacre at Fall Creek, Jessamyn West. Harcourt Brace Jovanovich, paper, 1986.
> This is the story of the trial following the massacre of Indians by five white men. **LA**

The Memory Sting, Chester G. Osborne. Macmillan, 1984.
> The migration of populations across the Bering Strait land bridge to North America is the historical setting of this story. **EA**

My Brother Sam Is Dead, James L. Collier and Christopher Collier. Macmillan, 1974. Scholastic, paper.
> A 16 year old joins the Continental Army against his parents' wishes. The sequels, **The Bloody Country** (Macmillan, 1977, Scholastic, paper +) and **The Winter Hero** (Macmillan, 1978, Scholastic, paper +), deal with the land dispute between Connecticut and Pennsylvania and Shays' Rebellion. **PA +**

No Hero for the Kaiser, Rudolf Frank. Lothrop, Lee & Shepard, 1986.
> Originally published in 1931 in German, this book is about the effects of World War I on a young hero who is forced to flee his Polish village to become part of the invading German Battery. **LA M**

Prairie Songs, Pam Conrad. Harper & Row, 1985.
> Louisa gains a better understanding of prairie life through contrasting the character and plain beauty of her mother with the frail loveliness of the new doctor's wife. **EA F**

The Road to Damietta, Scott O'Dell. Houghton Mifflin, 1985.
> This novel, set in a 13th century Italian village, is the story of a young girl whose love for Francis causes her to join him on the Fifth Crusade. **PA EA F +**

The Samurai's Tale, Erik Christian Haugaard. Houghton Mifflin, 1984.
> The son of a Samurai is orphaned and captured by powerful enemies of his father. He becomes a servant and must work his way up to Samurai. **PA**

Walking up a Rainbow, Theodore Taylor. Delacorte, 1986.
> A 14 year old orphan fights to save her California sheep ranch. **PA EA +**

The Wall, John Hersey. Knopf, 1961.
> The Jews of the Warsaw ghetto stand up against their oppressors. **LA**

The Witch of Blackbird Pond, Elizabeth George Speare. Houghton Mifflin, 1958. Dell, paper.
> The niece of a family in colonial Connecticut befriends the witch of Blackbird Pond and learns of the colonists' cruelty. **PA EA +**

You Never Knew Her As I Did!, Mollie Hunter. Harper & Row, 1981.
> In this novel based on the imprisonment of Mary, Queen of Scots, a 17 year old devises a plan for her escape. **PA EA +**

Humor

The Adventures of Huckleberry Finn, Mark Twain. 1884. Scholastic, paper, 1983.

> A classic adventure story in which Huck Finn journeys down the Mississippi with a runaway slave. **EA LA**

The Cat Ate My Gymsuit, Paula Danziger. Delacorte, 1974. Dell, paper.

> The first of Danziger's very funny books for adolescents deals with a 13 year old girl who is overweight and lonely. When she joins a fight to help a teacher, she finds friendship and her own identity. Danziger's other books include **Can You Sue Your Parents for Malpractice?** (1979 *), **The Divorce Express**(1986 *), **There's a Bat in Bunk Five** (1980 *), **It's an Aardvark-Eat-Turtle World** (1985 *), and **The Pistachio Prescription** (1978 *) (all published by Delacorte, Dell, paper). **PA EA ***

Discontinued, Julian E. Thompson. Scholastic, paper, 1986.

> Duncan learns he may be a target of the killer who killed his parents. The plot twists and turns until Duncan suggests that good and bad guys alike might just as well go home. **LA**

Half Nelson, Full Nelson, Bruce Stone. Harper & Row, 1985.

> Nelson's father is a second rate wrestler who runs off his wife and young daughter. Nelson and a friend go in search of them to try to restore the family. The characters and story are offbeat and funny. **EA LA**

The Snarkout Boys and the Avocado of Death, Daniel Pinkwater. Lothrop, Lee & Shepard, 1982. New American Library, paper.

> Winston and Walter, the Snarkout boys, go through a series of zany adventures. Readers who enjoy this book also will like **The Snarkout Boys and the Baconburg Horror** (Lothrop, Lee & Shepard, 1984, New American Library, paper *). **EA ***

The War Between the Pitiful Teachers & the Splendid Kids, Stanley Kiesel, Dutton, 1980. Avon, paper.

> A satire about a school called Scratchland where Skinny Malinky leads the kids in a war against the teachers. **Skinny Malinky Leads the War for Kidness** (Lodestar, 1985, Avon, paper) is the sequel. **PA EA ***

Who Put That Hair in My Toothbrush?, Jerry Spinelli. Little, Brown, 1984. Dell, paper.

> A humorous, heartwarming story of sibling rivalry. **PA * +**

Love and Romance

Acts of Love, Maureen Daly. Scholastic, 1986.

Parents and grandparents of young adults may remember reading Daly's first novel, **Seventeenth Summer** (Dodd, Mead, 1942, Archway, paper, 1968 *). In her second novel for young adults, Henrietta deals with changes in her hometown while developing a romantic interest in a mysterious young man with a past tied to her mother.   **EA F ***

Beginners' Love, Norma Klein. Dial, 1982.

Joel is shy, while Lela is aggressive. Their relationship progresses into the first sexual encounter for both of them.   **EA LA F ***

Cloudy-Bright, John Rowe Townsend. Lippincott, 1984. New American Library, paper.

Sam thinks he is interested in Jenny because she has the camera he needs to win the photography contest, but he soon realizes that it's more than her camera he's interested in.   **EA LA**

A Farewell to Arms, Ernest Hemingway. Scribner, paper, 1929.

This love story between an English nurse and a wounded American ambulance driver is set against the backdrop of the Italian campaign in World War I.   **LA**

The Fat Girl, Marilyn Sachs. Dutton, 1984. Dell, paper.

This is a beauty and the beast love story. Jeff and Norma, the beautiful people, are more than attracted to one another. But when Jeff makes 200 pound Ellen cry, his revulsion turns to fascination and he sets about transforming her.   **PA EA F**

Finding David Delores, Margaret Willey. Harper & Row, 1986.

Arly is obsessed with David and finally meets him but she learns more about herself and the value of friendship than love.   **EA F**

The Haunting of Safekeep, Eve Bunting. Lippincott, 1985.

This book weaves a love story and a ghost story. To qualify for a summer caretaking job, Sara and Dev agree to become a couple. They soon discover the ghost of Safekeep.   **EA F +**

Hey Kid! Does She Love Me?, Harry Mazer. Crowell, 1984.

An 18 year old boy in love with a 20 year old mother with a baby postpones his move to California to spend the summer with them.   **EA ***

I Stay Near You, M.E. Kerr. Harper & Row, 1985. Berkley, paper.

This romance novel covers three generations, tied together by a ring passed from one generation to another.   **EA LA F**

The Love Letters of J. Timothy Owens, Constance Greene. Harper & Row, 1986.

Tim finds an old trunk filled with love letters written by famous people. Inspired by the beauty of their language, he decides to write some of his own and send them to Sophie who is unaware of Tim and is convinced someone is sending her dirty letters.   **EA**

Motown and Didi: A Love Story, Walter Dean Myers. Viking, 1984.
Didi and Motown fall in love while trying to save Didi's brother from drug addiction. **EA** *

My Love, My Love, or the Peasant Girl, Rosa Guy. Holt, Rinehart & Winston, 1985.
This is a tragic romance about a beautiful black orphan who falls in love with a wealthy creole. **EA LA**

Roses, Barbara Cohen. Lothrop, Lee & Shepard, 1984. Scholastic, paper.
In this modern telling of beauty and the beast, Courtney becomes involved with the scarred owner of the florist shop in which she works. **EA LA F**

Sugar Blue, Vera Cleaver. Lothrop, Lee & Shepard, 1984. Dell, paper.
This is not a romance, but a love story about an 11 year old girl who takes care of her 4 year old niece. **PA F +**

Up in Seth's Room, Norma Fox Mazer. Delacorte, 1979. Dell, paper.
Seth is ready for a sexual relationship, but Finn is not. **LA F** *

What If They Saw Me Now?, Jean Ure. Delacorte, 1984. Dell, paper.
Jamie inadvertently becomes a ballet star when he reluctantly agrees to take the place of an injured dancer. He enjoys dancing, but does not want his friends to see him in tights. **EA**

When We First Met, Norma Fox Mazer. Macmillan, 1982. Scholastic, paper.
Jenny falls in love but is horrified to discover that her boyfriend's mother is the drunk driver who killed her sister two years earlier. They develop a relationship without the knowledge of their families, but feel guilty about their secretiveness. **EA LA F** *

Wuthering Heights, Emily Bronte. 1847. Bantam, paper, 1981.
This classic British romance depicting the tormented love of Heathcliff and Catherine is set on the rugged moors of the north of England. **LA**

The Year Summer Died, Patricia Lee Gauch. Putnam, 1985.
In this story of friendship and romance, Erin and Laurie have been friends for years, but when Laurie falls in love, Erin becomes the third wheel. **EA F** *

Music

I Will Call It Georgie's Blues, Suzanne Newton. Viking, 1983. Dell, paper.
Though the backdrop of this book is the jazz piano Neal plays to escape his family's problems, the book is really about family relationships and the problems caused by parents who expect perfection from their children. **EA**

Rock 'n' Roll Nights, Todd Strasser. Delacorte, 1982. Dell, paper.
This book and its sequel, **Turn It Up!** (Delacorte, 1984, Dell, paper *), are about a talented teenage musician who is trying to make it in the competitive world of rock 'n' roll. **EA** *

Mystery

The Arm of the Starfish, Madeleine L'Engle. Farrar, Straus & Giroux, 1965. Dell, paper.
Adam expects to spend a quiet summer working for a marine biologist but instead becomes involved with an international mystery. **EA +**

The Callender Papers, Cynthia Voigt. Macmillan, 1985. Fawcett, paper.
In this gothic novel Jean plans to spend her summer cataloging family papers in the old Callender home. She soon realizes the papers contain the key to the family mystery. **EA**

Doris Fein: Superspy, T. Ernesto Bethancourt. Holiday, 1980.
The Doris Fein mysteries (reminiscent of Nancy Drew mysteries) are about a modern girl in California. In this book she travels to New York and attempts to unravel an international mystery at the UN. **PA EA F ***

Down a Dark Hall, Lois Duncan. Little, Brown, 1974. Dell, paper.
In this gothic romance about ESP, four girls become prisoners in an exclusive girls' school. They realize why they were selected and how vulnerable they are. **EA F ***

Dragons in the Waters, Madeleine L'Engle. Farrar, Straus & Giroux, 1980. Dell, paper.
This novel, which combines murder, politics, and history to create suspense, is full of information on Venezuela, oil refining, and science. **EA LA +**

Footsteps: A Novel, Leon Garfield. Delacorte, 1980.
The setting for this 18th century mystery is William's father's bedroom. William attempts to fulfill his father's deathbed wish to find a man he swindled. **EA**

The Man in the Woods, Rosemary Wells. Dial, 1984. Scholastic, paper.
Helen finds her life threatened after she witnesses a crime. **EA**

The Seance, John Lowery Nixon. Harcount Brace Jovanovich, 1980. Dell, paper.
Sara, who lives with Lauren and her family, disappears after a seance and is presumed dead. When a second teenager is murdered, Lauren is sure she will be next. **EA**

Sirens and Spies, Janet Taylor Lisle. Bradbury, 1985. Berkley, paper.
Mary and Elsie become involved in a mystery surrounding their violin teacher, who had a mysterious past in occupied France during World War II. **EA F**

Slowly, Slowly I Raise the Gun, Jay Bennett. Avon, paper, 1983.
Chris receives an anonymous letter saying his mother was murdered and that he should seek revenge. **EA LA M ***

Sweet Whispers, Brother Rush, Virginia Hamilton. Putnam, 1982. Avon, paper.
Is Brother Rush really a ghost or a 15 year old learning to deal with her family's problems? This mystery is a worthwhile challenge for good readers. **EA +**

Tales of a Dead King, Walter Dean Myers. Morrow, 1983.
> There are many mysteries in this entertaining tale: a dead snake in a hotel room, a dagger whistling through the air, a missing archaeologist, and a lost treasure.   **PA** *

The Young Unicorns, Madeleine L'Engle. Farrar, Straus & Giroux, 1968. Dell, paper.
> A sinister gang of youths plots to destroy a former member and the blind musician he tutors.   **EA** +

Other Adults

Cheater and Flitter Dick, Robbie Branscum. Viking, 1983.
> Cheater, age 14, lives with her adopted father, Grabapple. Flitter Dick is her pet rooster. When a tornado destroys their home, Cheater comes to terms with her hatred for and jealousy of the Missus, and Grabapple overcomes his drinking problem.   **EA**

Far from Home, Ouida Sebestyen. Little, Brown, 1980. Dell, paper.
> After his mother dies, Salty sets out to find the father he has never known, only to find the love of his elderly grandmother.   **EA**

Figure of Speech, Norma Fox Mazer. Delacorte, 1973. Dell, paper.
> Tells of a child's love for her grandfather and her protection of him when other family members attempt to push him aside.   **PA** * +

The Great Gilly Hopkins, Katherine Paterson. Crowell, 1978. Avon, paper.
> Gilly is a foster child who has been thrown out of every foster home. Trotter vows to become family to her and succeeds in helping Gilly find herself.   **PA EA** *

LeRoy & the Old Man, W.E. Butterworth. Macmillan, 1980. Scholastic, paper.
> After witnessing a mugging, LeRoy flees to Mississippi to live with his grandfather. When the victim dies, LeRoy must decide if he will return to Chicago to testify.   **EA LA**

The Man Without a Face, Isabelle Holland. Lippincott, 1972. Harper & Row, paper.
> Chick feels rejected by his family and inferior to his sister. The "man without a face" tutors him for entrance exams for a prep school. They are attracted to one another and have a brief, sensitive, homosexual encounter. The book does not end with the encounter, but with Chuck's developing understanding of the meaning of love and affection.   **EA LA** *

Mighty Close to Heaven, Faye Gibbons. Morrow, 1985.
> Dave is left with his maternal grandparents after his mother's death. He sets out to find his father, but instead meets an elderly woman who helps him understand his grandparents.   **EA**

The Pigman, Paul Zindel. Harper & Row, 1968. Bantam, paper.
> Lorraine and John become friends with the elderly Mr. Pignati. Mr. Pignati dies of a heart attack after they have a wild party in his home while he is away. The teenagers must deal with their guilt. In **The Pigman's Legacy** (Harper & Row, 1980, Bantam, paper) John and Lorraine befriend another old man who is hiding in the Pigman's house. **EA LA**

Return to Bitter Creek, Doris Buchanan Smith. Viking, 1986.
> Lacey is the daughter of an unmarried woman who lives with an artist. They return to a North Carolina town to try to develop a relationship with Lacey's grandparents. **EA**

A Shadow Like a Leopard, Myron Levoy. Harper & Row, 1981. New American Library, paper.
> Ramon is a street punk and a gifted poet who forms a relationship with an elderly artist. **EA LA**

The Son of Someone Famous, M.E. Kerr. Harper & Row, 1974. New American Library, paper.
> For Adam, being the son of someone famous is not easy. He lives with his lonely, embittered grandfather. They both grow up emotionally and develop a sense of worth. **PA EA ***

What about Grandma?, Hadley Irwin. Macmillan, 1982. New American Library, paper.
> When grandmother refuses to live in a nursing home, Rhys and her mother spend the summer with her. It is a time of conflict and discovery for Rhys. **PA EA F ***

Parents

Back Home, Michelle Magorian. Harper & Row, 1984.
> Rusty is sent to the United States from England in 1940. When she returns home after World War II, the British find her rude and abrasive. No one wants to hear about the loving family she grew up with. **EA**

Dinky Hocker Shoots Smack, M.E. Kerr. Harper & Row, 1972. Dell, paper.
> This book is about overweight Dinky and her professional mother who is more concerned about her work than her daughter. The book's title is Dinky's cry for help. **PA EA**

IOUs, Ouida Sebestyen. Little, Brown, 1982. Dell, paper.
> Stowe is torn between his love for his mother and his desire to experiment with life. **EA**

Just the Two of Us, Hila Colman. Scholastic, paper, 1984.
> Samantha develops a relationship with her father that excludes all others. **EA F**

Of Love and Death and Other Journeys, Isabelle Holland. Lippincott, 1975.
> After her mother's sudden death, Meg is sent to live with the father she has never known. **EA F**

Ordinary People, Judith Guest. Viking, 1976. Ballantine, paper.
> Conrad must deal with his parents' reactions to his attempted suicide. **LA**

Sweetly Sings the Donkey, Vera Cleaver. Lippincott, 1985.
> The Snow family inherits property in Florida and attempts to build a home on its bare acreage. **PA EA**

Peer Relationships

All Together Now, Sue Ellen Bridgers. Knopf, 1979. Bantam, paper.
> A young tomboy befriends a mentally retarded man. **PA EA * +**

The Chocolate War, Robert Cormier. Pantheon, 1974. Dell, paper.
> This may be the most terrifying and thought provoking book ever written for young adults. Jerry stands up against a gang only to find that he is forced to stand alone. The sequel, **Beyond the Chocolate War** (Pantheon, 1986, Dell, paper), allows Jerry to resolve some of his bitterness. **LA**

Father Figure, Richard Peck. Viking, 1978. New American Library, paper.
> Jim finds his role as surrogate father to his 8 year old brother is threatened when they are forced to move in with their real father. **PA EA**

Hey, Dollface, Deborah Hautzig. Morrow, 1978.
> Explores the topic of lesbianism as two girls become concerned that their relationship is more than friendship. **EA LA**

Homecoming, Cynthia Voigt. Macmillan, 1981. Fawcett, paper.
> A 13 year old travels many miles with her younger brothers and sister searching for a home. The sequel, **Dicey's Song** (Macmillan, 1984, Fawcett, paper +) won the Newbery Award for its portrayal of the children's life on Maryland's Eastern Shore. **PA EA F +**

If I Love You, Am I Trapped Forever?, M.E. Kerr. Harper & Row, 1973. Dell, paper.
> An egocentric teenager learns about himself when he trades places with a boy he dislikes. **PA EA M ***

I Never Loved Your Mind, Paul Zindel. Harper & Row, 1970. Bantam, paper.
> This book contains Zindel's typical cast of madcap characters, in this case two high school dropouts seeking one another. **EA**

Long Time Between Kisses, Sandra Scoppettone. Harper & Row, 1982.
> A typical teenage girl confuses her feelings of self-negation and rebelliousness with love for a man with multiple sclerosis. **EA**

Lord of the Flies, William Golding. Putnam, 1954.
> English schoolboys marooned on an island attempt to set up their own society. The ending is horrifyingly realistic. **EA LA**

The Outsiders, S.E. Hinton. Viking, 1967. Dell, paper.
> In this book about teenage gangs the characters learn about the importance of life. Hinton's other books have similar plots: **That Was Then, This Is Now** (Viking, 1971, Dell, paper *), **Rumblefish** (Delacorte, 1975, Dell, paper *), and **Tex** (Delacorte, 1979, Dell, paper *). **EA * +**

Problem Novels

Abby, My Love, Hadley Irwin. Macmillan, 1985. New American Library, paper.
> In this sensitive story about incest, Abby's friend Chip doesn't understand her emotional ups and downs. **EA LA ***

About David, Susan Beth Pfeffer. Delacorte, 1980. Dell, paper.
> Lynn's friend David murders his parents and later kills himself. Through her journal, Lynn begins to deal with her anger, horror, and grief. **EA LA**

Angel Dust Blues, Todd Strasser. Coward, McCann & Geoghegan, 1979. Dell, paper.
> Alex is arrested for selling drugs to an undercover agent. The book, told in flashbacks, reveals how a normal high school student covers up his loneliness. **EA LA M ***

The Ape Inside Me, Kin Platt. Harper & Row, 1979. Bantam, paper.
> Ed is often violent. The book is particularly good for poor readers as its vocabulary is simple, while its message is mature. **EA LA M ***

Are You in the House Alone?, Richard Peck. Viking, 1976. Dell, paper.
> A young girl receives anonymous phone calls and obscene letters, then is raped by someone she knows. **EA LA ***

Bad Apple, Larry Bograd. Farrar, Straus & Giroux, 1982.
> Nicky is a victim of poverty and street life. He commits a burglary and is arrested. **EA LA M**

The Bigger Book of Lydia, Margaret Willey. Harper & Row, 1983.
> Lydia is small, but her problem is unimportant compared with Michelle's anorexia nervosa. **EA LA F**

The Boll Weevil Express, P.J. Petersen. Delacorte, 1983. Dell, paper.
> Three teenagers run away to San Francisco. **PA EA**

Center Line, Joyce Sweeney. Delacorte, 1984.
> Five brothers run away from their abusive, alcoholic father. The book's realistic language and sexual encounters are handled with sensitivity. **LA ***

Chloris and the Weirdos, Kin Platt. Bradbury, 1978. Bantam, paper.
> Two sisters react to their mother's divorce and subsequent new relationships. **PA EA F ***

Dead Birds Singing, Marc Talbert. Little, Brown, 1985.
> Matt must deal with the death of his mother and sister who were killed by a drunk driver. **EA**

A Different Kind of Love, Michael Borich. Holt, Rinehart & Winston, 1985.
  Weeble is betrayed by an adult she thought was a friend, but whose affection suggested sexual activity. **EA LA F**

The Family Trap, Hila Colman. Morrow, 1982.
  Three young people are forced to become emancipated minors after their father's death and mother's mental breakdown. **EA LA**

Final Grades, Anita Heyman. Dodd, Mead, paper, 1985.
  Three teenagers deal very differently with school pressures, both at home and at school. **EA LA F**

Forever, Judy Blume. Bradbury, 1975. Pocket Books, paper.
  Blume explores how young love leads to sexual activity. **EA LA F ***

Happy Endings Are All Alike, Sandra Scoppettone. Harper & Row, 1978. Dell, paper.
  Jaret is raped by a disturbed boy, leading to knowledge of her lesbian relationship with Peggy. **LA F**

If I Asked You, Would You Stay?, Eve Bunting. Lippincott, 1984.
  Though running away and suicide are prominent in this book, it is really about what trust can mean to a relationship. **LA**

I Was a Fifteen-Year-Old Blimp, Patti Stern. Harper & Row, 1985. New American Library, paper.
  A girl is so desperate for thinness and male attention that she begins a dangerous program of rapid weight loss. **PA EA F * +**

Jennie Kiss'd Me, Isabelle Holland. Fawcett, paper, 1985.
  Jill's mother dies and her father turns to alcohol. Jill is forced to take charge of her own life. **EA F**

The Kissimmee Kid, Vera Cleaver and Bill Cleaver. Lothrop, Lee & Shepard, 1981.
  Evie must decide whether to tell the truth about her brother-in-law's cattle rustling. **PA**

Nice Girl from Good Home, Fran Arrick. Bradbury, 1984. Dell, paper.
  Describes how family members react differently to a family crisis. **EA ***

One Fat Summer, Robert Lipsyte. Bantam, paper, 1978.
  Robert is overweight but conquers his problem when he gets a job mowing lawns. **Summer Rules** (Harper & Row, paper, 1981) is the sequel. **EA M * +**

The Pig-Out Blues, Jan Greenberg. Farrar, Straus & Giroux, 1982.
  Jodie overeats when she feels disappointed. Helpful friends get her on the right track. **PA EA F ***

The Question Box, Roberta Hughey. Delacorte, 1984.
  Anne Gilbert rebels against her father's rigidity. **EA**

Remembering the Good Times, Richard Peck. Delacorte, 1985. Dell, paper.
  This book traces the relationship of three close friends. No one recognizes the inner turmoil of one of them until it is too late; he commits suicide. **EA LA**

Risking Love, Doris Orgel. Dial, 1984. Fawcett, paper.
>Dinah is trying to deal with her parents' divorce and is unable to come to terms with the transient nature of love.   **EA LA F**

Something Beyond Paradise, Jan Slepian. Philomel, 1987.
>Three teenagers attempt to sort out the consequences of freedom and responsibility.   **EA LA**

To Be a Killer, Jay Bennett. Scholastic, paper, 1985.
>Paul considers killing his chemistry teacher after the teacher catches him stealing a copy of the final exam. Finally he reaches for help instead.   **EA ***

Weekend Sisters, Hila Colman. Morrow, 1985.
>On weekends Amanda must share her father with her new stepfamily. She decides to go away and let the new family sort out its problems.   **EA F**

Working On It, Joan Oppenheimer. Harcourt Brace Jovanovich, 1980. Dell, paper.
>Tracy hopes her shyness will vanish, but it does not. She takes command of her problem by signing up for a drama class.   **EA MA**

Science Fiction

Another Heaven, Another Earth, H.M Hoover. Viking, 1981.
>Survivors of an unsuccessful attempt to colonize another planet must choose between life on that doomed planet or on mechanized, overcrowded earth.   **PA EA +**

The Bell Tree, H.M. Hoover. Viking, 1982.
>Henny and her father search for an ancient civilization. The book is readable by younger adolescents but the questions it poses are not easily answered.   **PA EA**

Beyond Silence, Eleanor Cameron. Dutton, 1980. Dell, paper.
>Andy goes back in time and meets Deirdre.   **EA**

Beyond the Dark River, Monica Hughes. Macmillan, 1981.
>An Amish boy and an Indian girl survive a nuclear holocaust and venture into a destroyed city to seek information about medicines to save dying children.   **PA EA**

Blossom Culp and the Sleep of Death, Richard Peck. Delacorte, 1986.
>Blossom is haunted by an ancient Egyptian princess. With the help of a friend, Blossom restores the princess to her rightful place in history. Other books in the Blossom series are **The Ghost Belonged to Me** (Viking, 1987, Dell, paper * +), **Ghosts I Have Been** (Viking, 1987, Dell, paper * +), and **The Dreadful Future of Blossom Culp** (Delacorte, 1987, Dell, paper *).   **PA EA ***

Brave New World, Aldous Huxley. Harper & Row, paper, 1932.
>A classic story of a dehumanized future world.   **LA**

Deadeye Dick, Kurt Vonnegut. Delacorte, 1982. Dell, paper.
> Vonnegut offers his usual crop of madcap characters and humor mixed with the themes of inhumanity and technology gone wild. Older adolescents who enjoy this book may also enjoy Vonnegut's many other books.   **LA**

Devil on My Back, Monica Hughes. Macmillan, 1985. Bantam, paper.
> Personal computers are attached directly to people's brains.   **EA**

Dune, Frank Herbert. Chilton, 1965. Berkley, paper.
> A space fantasy that takes place on a desert planet. Mathematics whizzes are particularly fond of Herbert's books.   **LA**

Foundation, Isaac Asimov. Gnome, 1951. Ballantine, paper.
> The first of a series in which Hari Seldon creates the Foundations to preserve human culture during the dark ages after the collapse of the first galactic empire. The other books in the trilogy are **Foundation and Empire** (Gnome, 1983. Ballantine, paper) and **The Second Foundation** (Doubleday, 1983, Ballantine, paper).   **LA**

House of Stairs, William Sleator. Dutton, 1974. Scholastic, paper.
> Five young people are taken from state institutions to a place without walls, ceiling, or floor, but with endless stairs and a red machine that controls them.   **EA** * +

Interstellar Pig, William Sleator. Dutton, 1984. Bantam, paper.
> Barney's neighbors invite him to play a game in which competing aliens do extreme things to get a smiling pink pig.   **EA** * +

Keeper of the Isis Light, Monica Hughes. Macmillan, 1981.
> Olwen does not know how different she is from others on Isis until earth settlers come and she falls in love.   **EA**

The Martian Chronicles, Ray Bradbury. Doubleday, 1946. Bantam, paper.
> In this series of short tales, earthlings gain and lose Mars.   **EA LA**

Short Stories

Break of Dark, Robert Westall. Greenwillow, 1982.
> Macabre short stories about such things as a supernatural nude, a German pilot who keeps coming back to life, and a horse trough involved in purse snatching.   **EA LA**

Coming-and-Going Men: Four Tales, Paul Fleishman. Harper & Row, 1985.
> Stories about a traveling man who comes in contact with the little town of New Canaan, Vermont, in 1900.   **LA**

Early Sorrow: Ten Stories of Youth, edited by Charlotte Zolotow. Harper & Row, 1986.
> Stories dealing with a deeply traumatic moment in an adolescent's life.   **EA LA**

Eight Plus One, Robert Cormier. Pantheon, 1980. Bantam, paper.
>Each story is introduced with the author's thoughts about how and why it was created, making this a great tool for budding writers. **EA LA +**

Giving Birth to Thunder, Sleeping with His Daughter, Barry Lopex.
>Andrews, 1978. Avon, paper.
>A collection of 68 stories from the oral traditions of more than 40 Indian tribes. **EA LA +**

Imaginary Lands, edited by Robin McKinley. Greenwillow, 1986.
>The setting is the most important part of each story. **PA EA +**

Sixteen Short Stories by Outstanding Writers for Young Adults, edited by
>Donald R. Gallo. Delacorte, 1984. Dell, paper.
>All of the stories have memorable teenage characters. Also try **Visions: Nineteen Short Stories by Outstanding Writers for Young Adults** (Delacorte, 1987). **EA +**

Summer Girls, Love Boys & Other Short Stories, Norma Fox Mazer.
>Delacorte, 1982. Dell, paper.
>Stories about relationships that are not always what they seem. **EA F ***

To Break the Silence, Peter A. Barrett. Dell, 1986.
>Thirteen stories for younger adolescents. Most have adolescent protagonists. **PA +**

A Touch of Chill, Joan Aiken. Delacorte, 1980.
>These stories will keep young readers on the edge of their seats. This is a good choice for reluctant readers. **PA EA +**

A Very Brief Season, Barbara Girion. Scribner, 1984. Berkley, paper.
>Stories about the pain of adolescence. **EA F**

A Whisper in the Night: Tales of Terror and Suspense, Joan Aiken.
>Delacorte, 1984.
>This collection of suspense tales will intrigue most young readers. **PA EA +**

Social Issues

Brother in the Land, Robert Swindells. Holiday, 1985.
>Danny lives through a nuclear holocaust, then experiences the more poignant emotional devastation of the survivors. **EA LA**

The Changelings, Jo Sinclair. McGraw-Hill, 1955. Feminist Press, paper.
>Blacks unsuccessfully seek housing in a Jewish neighborhood. Judith first believes the blacks are the enemy until a black girl offers her protection when her status as gang leader is challenged. **EA LA F +**

The Cry of the Seals, Larry Weinberg. Bantam, paper.
>This book addresses the controversy of seal killing from the alternating perspectives of an environmentalist and a hunter. **EA LA +**

The Day They Came to Arrest the Book, Nat Hentoff. Delacorte, 1982. Dell, paper.
Three groups want to have **Huckleberry Finn** removed from the school library: blacks because it is racist, women because it is sexist, and parents because it is immoral. The community becomes polarized over the battle.
EA LA +

Find a Stranger, Say Good-Bye, Lois Lowry. Houghton Mifflin, 1978. Archway, paper.
Natalie is an adopted daughter who feels compelled to seek the identity of her biological parents. **EA F**

First Blood, David Morrell. Evan, 1972. Fawcett, paper.
A Vietnam veteran comes home scarred by the violence he experienced in the war. **LA**

Fiskadoro, Denis Johnson. Knopf, 1985.
This book is set long after a nuclear holocaust in the last remaining part of the United States. **EA LA**

God's Radar, Fran Arrick. Bradbury, 1983. Dell, paper.
A teenager is caught between the fundamentalism of the community and the humanism of her family. **EA LA ***

The Kolokol Papers, Larry Bograd. Farrar, Straus & Giroux, 1981. Dell, paper.
Lev's father, a major civil rights leader in the Soviet Union, is arrested. Lev is left in charge of his family and struggles to get a secret transcript of his father's trial. **EA LA +**

Los Alamos Light, Larry Bograd. Farrar, Straus & Giroux, 1983.
Maggie's father is invited to work as a physicist in Los Alamos in 1943. Secrecy surrounds their lives; the story shows how different family members handle the tension. **EA LA**

The Love Bombers, Gloria Miklowitz. Delacorte, 1980. Dell, paper.
Jenna searches for her brother Jeremy who has joined a group known as the Church of the World. The book attempts to give an objective view of religious cults. **EA LA**

A Matter of Principle, Susan Beth Pfeffer. Delacorte, 1982.
High school students print an underground paper, are suspended, and become involved in a legal battle to defend their First Amendment rights. **LA**

Night Talks, Patricia Lee Gauch. Putnam, 1983. Archway, paper.
Three female campers from different backgrounds attempt to become friends. **PA EA F**

Pride of the Peacock, Stephanie Tolan. Scribner, 1986. Ballantine, paper.
Whitney is terrified of a nuclear disaster and lashes out at others who do not seem to understand her concern. Eventually she learns to deal with life more optimistically. **EA +**

Separate Tracks, Jane Rogers. Faber, paper, 1985.

> Emma, who lives near frequent strikes and riots, attempts to deal with her guilt about her comfortable background by getting involved in "do good" causes. She falls in love with Orph and learns that their differences keep them on separate tracks. **LA F**

Simple Gifts, Joanne Greenberg. Holt, Rinehart & Winston, 1986.

> A government agency wants to turn the Fleuris' rundown farm into a tourist attraction. **EA**

A Sinless Season, Damon Galgut. Ball, 1982. Penguin, paper.

> The story takes place in a reformatory where four boys are involved in a wave of destructive impulses. Violence may make this book inappropriate for less mature readers. **LA**

Slake's Limbo, Felice Holman. Scribner, 1974. Dell, paper.

> Thirteen year old Aremis is alone in New York and makes his home in the subway. When an accident destroys the world he has built he finds the courage to launch a life above ground. **PA EA * +**

Steffie Can't Come Out to Play, Fran Arrick. Dutton, 1978. Dell, paper.

> Steffie runs away to become a model and becomes a prostitute. **EA LA ***

Talking in Whispers, James Watson. Knopf, 1984. Fawcett, paper.

> This novel deals with what happens to civil rights in a military dictatorship in Chile. **EA LA**

The War Between the Classes, Gloria Miklowitz. Delacorte, 1985. Dell, paper.

> A social studies class takes part in the Color Game, a four week experiment to help students understand the damage done by labeling and sterotyping. **EA**

The Wave, Morton Rhue (Todd Strasser). Delacorte, 1981. Dell, paper.

> A history teacher uses a teaching method called The Wave to introduce students to what it would be like to live under a fascist government. The experiment backfires when it moves beyond the classroom. **EA LA * +**

When the Stars Begin to Fall, James L. Collier. Delacorte, 1986.

> Harry sets out to expose a carpet factory that is polluting the river and meets resistance from everyone, including his family. **EA LA**

Sports

The Atami Dragons, David Klass. Scribner, 1984.

> Jerry believes this is the year the Midland Rats will win the baseball championship, but his dreams are dashed when he must travel to Japan with his father. He learns that baseball is an international sport when he joins the Atami Dragons. **PA M ***

Brogg's Brain, Kin Platt. Lippincott, 1981.

> Monty is the number three miler at Emerson High. Everyone believes he could be a better runner and he wonders if they are right. **EA ***

The Contender, Robert Lipsyte. Harper & Row, 1967. Harper & Row, paper.
> A young boxer learns that being a contender is more important than being a champion. **EA LA * +**

Halfback Tough, Thomas J. Dygard. Morrow, 1986.
> Football helps Joe change from a student who always violates the rules and looks down on others to one who is respected by peers and adults. **EA M**

Hoops, Walter Dean Myers. Delacorte, 1981. Dell, paper.
> Lonnie and his Harlem teammates learn about playing basketball (winning and losing) and about living from a former professional basketball player. **PA LA M ***

The Throwing Season, Michael French. Delacorte, 1980. Dell, paper.
> Indian is an outstanding shot putter. When asked to throw a competition, he refuses and is severely beaten, but fights back to win again. **EA**

Tournament Upstart, Thomas Dygard. Morrow, 1984.
> A team from a small high school enters a major basketball tournament. **EA M**

Zanboomer, R.R. Knudson. Harper & Row, 1978. Dell, paper.
> Zan is the star of a baseball team. Other books about Zan include **Zanballer** (Penguin, 1986 *), **Zanbanger** (Harper & Row, 1977 *), and **Zan Hagen's Marathon** (Farrar, Straus & Giroux, 1984, New American Library, paper *). **PA EA F ***

Suspense and Adventure

After the First Death, Robert Cormier. Pantheon, 1979. Avon, paper.
> A school bus is hijacked by an Arab terrorist. Readers get to know and understand the terrorist. The terrifying climax is thought provoking. **EA LA**

And Nobody Knew They Were There, Otto Salassi. Greenwillow, 1984.
> Jakey and his cousin attempt to solve a mystery that grownups cannot, stalk an elusive prey, and survive by their wits. **PA EA M * +**

Brothers of the Heart, Joan Blos. Scribner, 1985.
> Fourteen year old handicapped Shem runs away from home and joins a trading expedition. He finds himself alone and lost as winter approaches. **PA EA**

The Bumblebee Flies Anyway, Robert Cormier. Knopf, 1983. Dell, paper.
> A psychological thriller in which a 16 year old becomes an experimental subject in a hospital treating the chronically ill. **EA LA**

Crime and Punishment, Fyodor Dostoyevsky. 1866. Bantam, paper.
> A Russian student commits robbery and murder and is hounded by his own guilt and a suspicious police inspector. **LA**

The Executioner, Jay Bennett. Avon, paper, 1982.
> Bruce recalls the car accident he caused that killed his friend. His reflection makes him realize that someone is out to kill him. **EA ***

Finders Weepers, Katie Letcher Lyle. Coward, McCann & Geoghegan, 1982. Scholastic, paper.
> Lee stumbles on a famous treasure hidden in a cave. She concludes that it carries a curse, for each time someone takes something from it tragedy strikes. **EA** *

Frankenstein, Mary Shelley. 1818. Bantam, paper.
> A young scientist creates a monster who wreaks havoc and destroys himself. **LA**

The Ghost-Maker, Kathleen Kilgore. Houghton Mifflin, 1984. Avon, paper.
> Leeson is expelled from boarding school and goes to live with his grandmother in a town that is a haven for spiritualists. **EA**

I Am the Cheese, Robert Cormier. Pantheon, 1977. Dell, paper.
> Adam starts a bicycle trip to find his hospitalized father. Throughout the book the reader learns the horrifying secrets of Adam and his family. **EA LA**

Killing Mr. Griffin, Lois Duncan. Little, Brown, 1978. Dell, paper.
> A group of high school students sets out to scare a strict high school English teacher, but their prank turns into horror. **EA** * +

Liar, Liar, Lawrence Yep. Morrow, 1983. Avon, paper.
> Marsh, a known practical joker, is killed in a car accident in which his friend Sean is a passenger. Sean and Marsh's sisters attempt to find out if someone tampered with the brakes. **EA**

Locked in Time, Lois Duncan. Little, Brown, 1985. Dell, paper.
> Nore's mother dies and Nore goes to live with her father and stepfamily. She soon realizes that a dream of her mother warning that she and her father are in danger is more than her resentment over her father's remarriage. **EA**

Nobody Else Can Walk It for You, P.J. Petersen. Dell, paper, 1986.
> A strong young woman is responsible for getting a group of teenagers to safety. **EA**

On the Edge, Gillian Cross. Holiday, 1985.
> Tug is kidnapped by a terrorist group that has mastered the art of mind games. **EA**

Out of Sight, Out of Mind, Chester Aaron. Lippincott, 1985. Bantam, paper.
> Teenage twins are able to communicate mentally. Their combined powers allow them to move heavy objects. When their plane is struck by a missile they survive and are caught up in international intrigue. **EA**

Pursuit, Michael French. Delacorte, 1982. Dell, paper.
> A hiking trip in an isolated area ends in a clash of wills among the four hikers. **EA LA**

A Rumor of Otters, Deborah Savage. Houghton Mifflin, 1986.
> Alexa lives on an isolated sheep station in New Zealand. She leaves home to search for otters. **EA F**

Shadow on the Snow, Bill Wallace. Holiday, 1985.
> A city boy moves to the country and learns to fish, explore the wilds, and ride horses. These new skills prepare him for a rescue mission during a blizzard. **PA EA M**

The Shining, Stephen King. Doubleday, 1978. New American Library, paper.
The Torrance family, including 5 year old Daniel who has ESP, must fight
demonic forces in the hotel for which they are caretakers.   **LA**

Sweet Friday Island, Theodore Taylor. Scholastic, paper, 1984.
On a trip to a Mexican island, Peg and her father discover that a madman is
attempting to kill them.   **EA**

The Truth Trap, Frances Miller. Dutton, 1980. Fawcett, paper.
Matt is a suspect in the murder of his deaf sister. He is befriended by a
detective who believes he is innocent. Readers interested in Matt's problems
may want to read **Aren't You the One Who—?** (Fawcett, 1985) and
Losers and Winners (Fawcett, 1986).   **EA**

Wilderness Peril, Thomas Dygard. Morrow, 1985.
On a canoe trip in Minnesota, Todd and Mike find money left by a hijacker.
They realize they must get out before he returns.   **EA LA M**

Chapter 7

Nonfiction Kids Love

Many teens, particularly boys, prefer nonfiction to fiction. Since school experience with nonfiction usually is limited to textbooks and reference books, many students are not exposed to nonfiction books written specifically for them.

The amount of nonfiction for adolescents increases each year. This annotated bibliography is organized into sections to help you select books. For an explanation of the bibliographic information that appears with each entry, see Chapter 6.

Animals

Born Free: A Lioness of Two Worlds, Joy Adamson. Pantheon, paper, 1960.
 A moving story of the lioness Elsa, told by a woman who loved her. **EA LA +**
Dance of the Wolves, Roger Peters. McGraw-Hill, 1985. Ballantine, paper.
 A young researcher's personal story of three winters studying the wolves of northern Michigan. **PA EA LA**

Dr. Wildlife: The Crusade of a Northwoods Veterinarian, Rory C. Foster.
Watts, 1985. Ballantine, paper.
Depicts one man's love of animals. **EA LA**

Incident at Hawk's Hill, Allan Eckert. Little, Brown, 1971. Dell, paper.
A delightful story about a 6 year old boy cared for by a badger. **EA LA * +**

Max, the Dog That Refused to Die, Kyra Petrovskaya Wayne. Alpine, 1979.
Bantam, paper.
Max, a Doberman, is separated from his family in Yosemite and seriously
injured, but he refuses to die. **PA * +**

Secret Go the Wolves, R.D. Lawrence. Holt, Rinehart & Winston, 1980.
Ballantine, paper.
The author tells how he raised two wolf cubs to maturity. **EA LA**

The Zoo That Never Was: The Reluctant Zoo Keeper, R.D. Lawrence. Holt,
Rinehart & Winston, 1981.
The author and his wife face resistance from local governments when they try
to care for injured and helpless animals. **EA LA**

The Arts

Black Music in America: A History Through Its People, James Haskins.
Crowell, 1987.
The author of **Black Theater in America** (Crowell, 1982) discusses the
development of black music from the time of slavery to the 1980s. **EA LA**

Chapters: My Growth as a Writer by Lois Duncan. Little, Brown, 1982.
This autobiography of a popular young adult writer appeals to adolescents
who hope to have a career in writing. **EA LA F**

Duke Ellington, James Lincoln Collier. Oxford, 1987.
This followup to **Louis Armstrong: An American Genius** (Oxford, 1983)
deals mainly with Ellington's band and music. **EA LA**

Nothing but the Best: The Struggle for Perfection at the Juilliard School,
Judith Kogan. Random House, 1987.
The story of the most prestigious school for the arts in America told from the
perspective of former students. **EA LA**

Reaching for Dreams: A Ballet from Rehearsal to Opening Night, Susan
Kuklin. Lothrop, Lee & Shepard, 1987.
A beautifully photographed, vivid description of the ballet that appeals to
younger adolescents who dream of a career in ballet. **PA EA ***

To All Gentleness: William Carlos Williams, The Doctor Poet, Neil
Baldwin. Macmillan, 1984.
A beautifully told biography of a remarkable man who combined his love of
medicine with his love for poetry. **EA LA +**

Uncommon Eloquence: A Biography of Angna Enters, Dorothy Mandel. Arden, 1986.
Angna Enters was a gifted writer, dancer/mime, set designer, and artist from the 1920s through the 1970s. This story may inspire older adolescent girls.
LA F

Winter Season, Toni Bently. Random House, 1982. Vintage, paper.
The story of the New York City Ballet's winter season of 1980-1981 from the perspective of one of its ballerinas. **EA LA F**

Biography and Autobiography

American Dreams: Lost and Found, Studs Terkel. Pantheon, 1980. Ballantine, paper.
Minibiographies of the great, the near great, and the not so great told by one of America's foremost oral anthropologists. **LA**

Anne Frank, the Diary of a Young Girl, Anne Frank. Doubleday, 1946. (Now available in many editions, under several different titles, from numerous publishers.)
This is the day by day account of a young Jewish girl forced to hide in an attic from June 1942 to August 1944. **EA F**

Blue Hills Remembered: A Recollection, Rosemary Sutcliff. Morrow, 1984.
The author traces her beginnings from a lonely child of a British naval officer to a gifted writer of historical fiction. **EA LA F +**

Boston Boy, Nat Hentoff. Knopf, 1986.
Writer Nat Hentoff explores the impact on his writing of his years in Boston, from early childhood to early adulthood. **LA**

The First Woman Doctor, Rachel Baker. Scholastic, paper, 1987.
An easy to read biography of Elizabeth Blackwell, who practiced medicine in the 19th century. **PA ***

Grace in the Wilderness, Aranka Siegal. Farrar, Straus & Giroux, 1985. Signet, paper.
This sequel to **Upon the Head of the Goat** (Farrar, Straus & Giroux, 1981, New American Library, paper.) is the story of Piri Davidowitz's life after she was liberated from Auschwitz. Since it covers her adolescent years, it is of particular interest to adolescents. **EA LA**

Hold On to Love, Mollie Hunter. Harper & Row, 1984.
This wonderful sequel to **A Sound of Chariots** (Harper, 1972, * +) reads more like a novel than an autobiography of the life of this well known British author. **EA LA * +**

Home Before Night, Hugh Leonard. Atheneum, 1980.
An autobiographical account of adolescence in Dublin during the 1930s. **LA**

I Am Fifteen—and I Don't Want to Die, Christine Arnothy. Dutton, 1950. Scholastic, paper.
An autobiographical account of a young woman who survived the Hungarian Holocaust.   **EA LA +**

I Know Why the Caged Bird Sings, Maya Angelou. Random House, 1970. Bantam, paper.
This first volume in the autobiography of a gifted black singer, dancer, and poet is particularly appropriate for adolescents because it recounts Angelou's childhood and early adolescence. Some parts are disturbing and graphic.   **LA F**

Isaac Bashevis Singer: The Story of a Storyteller, Paul Kresh. Dutton, 1984.
Traces Singer's life from his childhood in Poland to his 1978 Nobel Prize for literature.   **PA EA**

The Right Stuff, Tom Wolfe. Farrar, Straus & Giroux, 1979. Bantam, paper.
The story of the early NASA test pilots.   **EA LA**

Singing Creek Where the Willows Grow, Benjamin Hoff. Ticknor, 1986. Warner, paper.
The diary of a magically gifted 7 year old girl who wanders the woodlands.   **PA EA * +**

Careers

American Almanac of Jobs and Salaries, John Wright. Avon, paper, 1987.
This frequently updated work provides information on career and job opportunities.   **EA LA**

The Children of Santa Clara, Elizabeth Marek. Viking, 1987.
The sensitive story of a young woman who discovers herself through her work with special children.   **EA LA ***

Self-Made Women: Twelve of America's Leading Entrepreneurs Talk about Success, Self-Image, and the Superwoman, Diane Jennings. Taylor, paper, 1984.
Examines the careers of twelve successful women.   **LA F**

Working, Studs Terkel. Pantheon, 1974. Ballantine, paper.
The premier oral history of working people in America.   **EA LA**

Working Kids on Working, Sheila Cole. Lothrop, Lee & Shepard.
A collection of interviews with working kids.   **PA EA**

Ethnic

Black Americans: A History in Their Own Words, edited by Milton Meltzer. Crowell, 1984.

Meltzer uses the writings of hundreds of blacks to help young readers understand the black experience in America.   **PA EA LA**

Black Like Me, John Howard Griffin. Houghton Mifflin, 1977. New American Library, paper.

The classic story of a white man who disguises himself as a black and travels through the deep south.   **LA**

The Chinese of America, Jack Chen. Harper & Row, 1982.

Examines the role of the Chinese in American history. A comprehensive historical and social account appropriate for mature readers.   **LA**

The Education of Little Tree, Forest Carter. Delacorte, 1976.

A beautiful account of 5 year old Little Tree, who goes to live with his Cherokee grandparents in a Tennessee log cabin during the 1930s.   **PA EA LA * +**

Farewell to Manzanar, Jeanne Wakatsuki Houston and James Houston. Bantam, paper, 1974.

The moving story of a young Japanese girl's life in a relocation camp during World War II.   **EA LA ***

Freedom Train: The Story of Harriet Tubman, Dorothy Sterling. Scholastic, paper, 1987.

The story of Tubman, who risked her life to help others escape to freedom.   **PA EA ***

Indian Chiefs, Russell Freedman. Holiday House, 1987.

A beautifully illustrated, well documented narrative of six Indian chiefs, including Red Cloud and Sitting Bull.   **PA EA LA ***

Manchild in the Promised Land, Claude Brown. Macmillan, 1965. New American Library, paper.

The autobiography of childhood in Harlem by a man who pulled himself up from drugs, crime, and poverty.   **LA**

Roots, Alex Haley. Doubleday, 1976. Dell, paper.

The seven generation story of a family from its roots in West Africa to the plantations of pre-Civil War America.   **EA LA +**

To Be a Slave, Julius Lester. Dial, 1968. Scholastic, paper.

Graphically describes the experiences of men and women who lived as slaves.   **LA**

Handicaps and Illness

AIDS: The Ultimate Challenge, Elisabeth Kübler-Ross. Macmillan, paper, 1987.

Includes frank discussions with friends, families, and AIDS victims.   **EA LA**

Brian's Song, William Blinn. Bantam, paper, 1972.
Tells of football star Brian Piccolo's life and career, cut short by cancer. **EA LA** *

Death Be Not Proud: A Memoir, John Gunther. Harper & Row, 1949. Harper & Row, paper.
A much loved book written as a tribute to the author's adolescent son who died of cancer. **EA LA** +

If We Could Hear the Grass Grow, Eleanor Craig. Simon & Schuster, 1983. New American Library, paper.
Recounts the author's experience with severely disturbed children during a summer at Camp Hopewell. **EA LA**

Jordi, Theodore Isaac Rubin. Macmillan, paper, 1987.
A moving portrait of a disturbed child told by a well known psychiatrist.

Lisa & David, Theodore Isaac Rubin. Macmillan, paper, 1987.
The story of two disturbed children told by the psychiatrist who worked with them. **EA LA**

One Child, Torey L. Hayden. Avon, paper, 1982.
A story of emotionally disturbed children told with insight and compassion by their teacher. **EA LA**

Questions and Answers on AIDS, Lyn Frumkin and John Leonard. Avon, paper, 1987.
Unbiased answers to nearly 200 questions dealing with all aspects of AIDS. **EA LA**

Robyn's Book, A True Diary, Robyn Miller. Scholastic, 1986. Ballantine, paper.
Robyn, who died of cystic fibrosis at the age of 21, tells her own story. **PA EA LA F**

The Sick of Being Sick Book, Bob Stine and Jane Stine. Scholastic, paper, 1982.
A humorous book about dealing with all kinds of illness. **PA**

The Story of My Life, Helen Keller. Doubleday, 1954. Dell, paper.
The remarkable story of a woman who overcame deafness and blindness. **PA EA LA** +

History and Government

The American Revolutionaries: A History in Their Own Words, 1750-1800, edited by Milton Meltzer. Crowell, 1987.
A fascinating account of the Revolution told by the people who experienced it. **PA EA LA** +

The Americans: The Colonial Experience, 1985; **The Americans: The National Experience,** 1985; **The Americans: The Democratic Experience,** 1984. Daniel J. Boorstin. Random House, paper.
These books have won numerous prizes for their accurate and readable portrayal of American history. **LA**

Brother, Can You Spare a Dime? The Great Depression, 1929-1933,
Milton Meltzer. New American Library, paper, 1977.
First hand accounts woven into the history of the Depression.
The Eagle and the Dragon, Don Lawson. Crowell, 1985.
Traces the 200 year history of America's relationship with China. **EA LA**
Eyes on the Prize: America's Civil Rights Years, 1954-1965, Juan Williams.
Viking, 1987.
A companion volume to a PBS television series that chronicles the Civil
Rights movement. **EA LA**
If I Die in a Combat Zone, Tim O'Brien. Dell, paper, 1987.
A powerful, graphic book about one soldier's experiences in Vietnam. **LA**
The Jews: Story of a People, Howard Fast. Dell, paper, 1978.
A wonderfully illustrated and photographed account tracing the 4,000 year
history of the Jewish people. **MA LA**
Kent State: What Happened and Why, James A. Michener. Fawcett, 1978.
Ballantine, paper.
A fascinating, expertly written account of the most horrifying incident of the
Vietnam protest era. **LA**
Lines of Battle, Annette Tapert. Times, 1987.
A series of letters written by World War II GIs. **EA LA**
Never to Forget: The Jews of the Holocaust, Milton Meltzer. Dell, paper,
1976.
A carefully researched and compassionate account of the real people of the
Holocaust. **PA EA LA * +**
The Pantheon Documentary Comic Books Series. Includes **Trotsky for
Beginners,** Tariq Ali, 1980; **Freud for Beginners,** Richard Appignanesi
and Oscar Zarate, 1979; **Lenin for Beginners,** Richard Appignanesi, 1979;
Economics for Beginners, Bernard Caravan, 1982; **Ecology for
Beginners,** Stephen Croall, 1981; **Capitalism for Beginners,** Robert
Lekachman, 1981; **Einstein for Beginners,** Michael McGuinness and Joe
Schwartz, 1979; **Darwin for Beginners,** Jonathan Miller, 1982; **Mao for
Beginners,** Rius, 1980; **Marx for Beginners,** Rius, 1980; and **Marx's
Kapital for Beginners,** David Smith, 1982. Pantheon, paper.
This clever series unites illustrations with humorous text about highly
sophisticated subjects. **PA ***
The Rise and Fall of Adolf Hitler, William L. Shirer. Random House, paper,
1984.
An American correspondent in Berlin during the Third Reich writes a
personal account of the Nazi movement. **EA LA**
Scalded to Death by Steam, Katie Letcher Lyle. Algonquin, 1983.
This unusual book is about little known railroad disasters and the ballads
written about them. **EA LA**
Ten Days That Shook the World, John Reed. Random House, 1960.
New American Library, paper.
A first person account of the ten days that followed the Bolshevik takeover of
Russia. **EA LA**

How to Books

All about Your Money, Dan Fitzgibbon. Macmillan, 1984.
> A good book to assist adolescents in learning how to handle their money.   **PA EA LA** *

City Safaris: A Sierra Club Explorer's Guide to Urban Adventures for Grownups and Kids, Carolyn Shaffer and Erica Fielder. Sierra Club, 1987.
> A guide to looking at cities through people, parks, and imaginative activities.   **PA EA LA** *

College Admissions: Cracking the System, Adam Robinson and John Katzman. Random House, paper, 1987.
> A straightforward guide to selection, application, and acceptance to college.   **LA**

How to Study, Harry Maddox. Fawcett, 1985. Ballantine, paper.
> Designed to help students develop more productive study habits and more efficient thinking.   **EA LA**

I Hate School: How to Hang In and When to Drop Out, Claudine G. Wirths and Mary Bowman-Kruhm. Crowell, 1986.
> An appropriate book for kids who are thinking of dropping out of school. It gives good advice on how to survive in school, without promising success. **PA EA LA** *

Losing Someone You Love: When a Brother or Sister Dies, Elizabeth Richter. Putnam, 1986.
> A frank, helpful guide dealing with sorrow, fear, loneliness, and anger.   **PA EA LA**

The Mentor Guide to Writing Term Papers and Reports, William C. Paxson. New American Library, paper, 1987.
> A student oriented guide that includes sample papers, stylistic tips, and hints for all stages of paper writing.   **MA LA**

Pack Up and Paint with Oils, Tom Robb. Knopf, 1987.
> A colorful guide for would be artists.   **PA EA LA**

Safe, Strong, and Streetwise, Helen Benedict. Atlantic, 1986.
> This is one of those books we wish adolescents did not need. It discusses the dangers of the streets and helps teens deal with them.   **PA EA LA**

Scholastic A+ Guides including **The A+ Guide to Good Grades,** Louise and Doug Colligan, 1984; **The A+ Guide to Book Reports,** Louise Colligan, 1984; **The A+ Guide to Research and Term Papers,** Louise Colligan, 1984; **The A+ Guide to Taking Tests,** Louise Colligan, 1984; **The A+ Guide to Good Writing,** Dianne Teitel Rubins, 1984; and **The A+ Guide to Better Vocabulary,** Vicki Tyler, 1985. Scholastic, paper.
> Helpful advice for students.   **PA EA LA** *

Writing Your Own Plays: Creating, Adapting, Improvising, Carol Korty. Scribner, 1986.
> A helpful guide for budding playwrights.   **EA LA**

Humor

All Creatures Great and Small, 1972; **All Things Bright and Beautiful,**
1975; **All Things Wise and Wonderful,** 1977; and **The Lord God Made
Them All,** 1981, James Herriot. St. Martin. Bantam, paper.
Wonderfully funny accounts of life as a Yorkshire, England, veterinarian.
EA LA +

Belles on Their Toes, 1984; **Cheaper by the Dozen,** 1963. Frank B. Gilbreth,
Jr. and Ernestine Gilbreth Carey. Bantam, paper.
Delightfully funny books about the Gilbreth family. **PA EA * +**

The Boat Who Wouldn't Float, Farley Mowat. Little, Brown, 1970. Bantam,
paper.
An adventure story about the people of Newfoundland and the
sea. **EA LA +**

The Dog Who Wouldn't Be, Farley Mowat. Little, Brown, 1957. Bantam, paper.
The story of Mowat's boyhood with Mutt. **EA LA +**

Teenage Romance: Or How to Die of Embarrassment, Delia Ephron. Viking,
1981. Ballantine, paper.
Humorous advice for teens experiencing their first romance. **EA LA F**

Math, Computers, and Puzzles

A Computer Dictionary for Kids and Other Beginners, David Fay Smith.
Ballantine, paper, 1984.
A dictionary made easy by its cartoon illustrations of difficult concepts and
procedures. **PA EA LA ***

Mazes and Mysteries, Leonore Klein. Scholastic, paper, nd.
A challenging collection of puzzles designed to help preadolescents develop
spatial perception and logic. **PA**

Realm of Algebra, 1981; **Realm of Numbers,** 1981, Isaac Asimov. Ballantine,
paper.
A prolific science fiction writer explains the whys and wherefores of algebra
and mathematics. **EA LA**

Super Puzzle Challenge, Joe Claro. Scholastic, paper, nd.
Challenging crosswords, acrostics, word finds, and more. **PA**

Tim Hartnell's Giant Book of Computer Games, Tim Hartnell. Ballantine,
paper, 1984.
This book, along with **Tim Hartnell's Second Giant Book of Computer
Games** (Ballantine, paper, 1984), has everything a computer game enthusiast
could want. **PA EA LA ***

**Timid Virgins Make Dull Company and Other Puzzles, Pitfalls, and
Paradoxes,** Dr. Crypton. Viking, 1985.
Puzzles and games for able and less able adolescents. **EA LA**

Myths, Legends, and Parascience

Ancient Myths, Norma Lorre Goodrich. New American Library, paper, nd.
    A vivid retelling of myths of Greece, India, Egypt, Rome, Crete, Persia, and
    Sumer.   **LA**
Beowulf, adapted by Rosemary Sutcliff. Smith, 1984.
    A retelling of the classic story of Beowulf and the monster Grendel.
    PA EA LA
Communion: A True Story, Whitley Strieber. Avon, paper, 1987.
    A true story about an individual who experienced an unexplained
    phenomenon.   **EA LA**
The Man Who Wanted Seven Wives, Katie Letcher Lyle. Algonquin, 1986.
    A book based on a murder mystery that was supposedly solved by the
    testimony of a ghost.   **EA LA**
Medieval Myths, Norma Lorre Goodrich. New American Library, paper, 1977.
    Myths from Scandinavia, Wales, France, Austria, Russia, and Spain.   **LA**
Mythology, Edith Hamilton. Little, Brown, 1942. New American Library, paper.
    A brief reference book for Greek, Roman, and Norse myths.   **EA LA**
The Sword in the Stone, T.H. White. Dell, paper, 1985.
    Chronicles the young life and adventures of the boy who became King
    Arthur.   **PA EA +**
They Dance in the Sky: Native American Star Myths, Jean Guard Monroe
    and Ray A. Williamson. Houghton Mifflin, 1987.
    A collection of American Indian myths dealing with stars.   **PA EA LA * +**
The UFO Conspiracy: The First Forty Years, Jenny Randles. Blandford, 1987.
    A historical account in which Randles contends there has been a cover up
    regarding UFOs.   **EA LA**

Personal and Family Problems

Boys and Sex; Girls and Sex, Wardell B. Pomeroy. Delacorte, 1981. Dell, paper.
    Revised editions of books designed to tell boys and girls and their parents
    what they need to know about growing up and modern sex roles.   **EA LA**
The Boys' and Girls' Book about Divorce, Richard A. Gardner. Aronson,
    1983. Bantam, paper.
    Based on thirteen years of therapeutic work with divorced parents and their
    children.   **PA**
Dear Bobby Simpson, Bobby Simpson. Dell, paper, 1984.
    Bobby Simpson is the preadolescent "Dear Abby." This is a compilation of his
    columns from **The Boston Herald.**   **PA**
800-COCAINE, Mark S. Gold. Bantam, paper, 1984.
    A complete guide to America's fastest growing drug problem.   **EA LA**

It Won't Happen to Me: Teenagers Talk about Pregnancy, Paula McGuire. Delacorte, 1983. Dell, paper.
> Fifteen adolescents talk frankly about pregnancy and motherhood. **PA EA LA F**

Let's Eat Right to Keep Fit, 1970; **Let's Stay Healthy,** 1983, Adelle Davis (edited and expanded by Ann Gildroy). New American Library, paper.
> Popular guides for eating well and staying healthy. **EA LA**

Loving Each Other, 1985; **Living, Loving, and Learning,** 1982; **Love,** 1982, Leo F. Buscaglia. Holt, Rinehart & Winston. Ballantine, paper.
> Sensitive, thought provoking books dealing with love, life, and relationships. **LA**

Sex, Drugs, and AIDS, Oralee Wachter. Bantam, paper, 1987.
> Based on a highly acclaimed film. Answers crucial questions for teens and their parents. **PA EA LA**

Teen Pregnancy: The Challenges We Faced, The Choices We Made, Donna Ewy and Rodger Ewy. New American Library, paper, 1985.
> A frank guide on childbirth and parenting for pregnant teenagers. **PA EA LA F**

Too Fat, Too Thin? Do You Have a Choice?, Caroline Arnold. Morrow, 1984.
> An information packed book dealing with the variety of eating problems found in adolescent girls. **PA LA F**

Why Am I So Miserable If These Are the Best Years of My Life?, Andrea B. Eagan. Lippincott, 1976. Avon, paper.
> Commonsense advice for teenage girls on hygiene, menstruation, birth control, pregnancy, boys, and legal rights. **PA EA LA F**

Poetry

The Break Dance Kids: Poems of Sport, Motion, and Locomotion, 1985; **The Sidewalk Racer and Other Poems of Sports and Motion,** 1977, Lillian Morrison. Lothrop, Lee & Shepard.
> Morrison is a master at catching motion and sports in poetry. **PA EA LA * +**

Bring Me All Your Dreams, edited by Nancy Larrick. Evans, 1980.
> Fifty-six dream poems. **PA EA LA * +**

Class Dismissed! High School Poems, 1982; **Class Dismissed: More High School Poems,** 1986, Mel Glenn. Houghton Mifflin.
> Poems that catch the essence of the school experience. **PA EA * +**

Don't Forget to Fly, edited by Paul Janeczko. Bradbury, 1981.
> Modern poems that reflect a range of human emotions. Other works by Janeczko include **Going Over to Your Place: Poems for Each Other** (Bradbury, 1987); **Pocket Poems: Selected for a Journey** (Bradbury, 1985); **Postcard Poems: A Collection of Poems for Sharing** (Bradbury, 1979); and **Strings: A Gathering of Family Poems** (Bradbury, 1984). **PA EA LA ***

The First Wave: Women Poets in America, 1915-1945, William Drake.
Macmillan, paper, 1987.
Contains poems of some of the greatest women poets of this century with
biographies of each poet. **EA LA +**

A Green Place, compiled by William J. Smith. Delacorte, 1982.
A collection of 20th century poetry compiled to demonstrate how poets use
language to heighten experience. **EA LA +**

I Am Phoenix: Poems for Two Voices, Paul Fleischman. Harper & Row, 1985.
Poems written to be read aloud by two readers at once. **EA LA**

If I Were in Charge of the World and Other Worries, Judith Viorst.
Macmillan, paper, 1984.
A delightful collection of poetry about the preadolescent experience. **PA * +**

A Latch Against the Wind, Victoria Forrester. Macmillan, 1985.
Poems about emotions, poetry, dawn, seasons, fairies, and nature. **LA**

Love Is Like the Lion's Tooth: An Anthology of Love Poems, compiled by
Frances McCullough. Harper & Row, 1984.
A collection of poems dealing with the effects and stages of love. **EA LA**

Love Lines: Poetry in Person, Betsy Hearne. Macmillan, 1987.
Love poems for adolescents. **PA EA LA ***

Monkey Puzzle and Other Poems, Myra Cohn Livingston. Atheneum, 1984.
Short poems about trees for children and adolescents. **EA LA**

O Frabjous Day: Poetry for Holidays and Celebrations, collected by Myra
Cohn Livingston. Macmillan, 1977.
A wonderful collection of poems to help celebrate nearly every
holiday. **PA EA LA * +**

Rainbows Are Made: Poems by Carl Sandburg, collected by Lee Bennett
Hopkins. Harcourt Brace Jovanovich, 1984.
A short anthology that makes Sandburg's poetry accessible to all readers.
Other collections by Hopkins include **My Mane Catches the Wind:
Poems about Horses** (Harcourt Brace Jovanovich, 1979), **Munching:
Poems about Eating** (Little, Brown, 1985), and **A Song in Stone: City
Poems** (Crowell, 1983). **PA EA LA * +**

Saturday's Children: Poems of Work, edited by Helen Plotz. Greenwillow,
1982.
Poems dealing with the emotions of work. **LA +**

Those Who Ride the Night Wind, Nikki Giovanni. Morrow, paper, 1983.
Upbeat, warm poems discussing the black experience through the eyes of a
gifted black poet. **LA +**

Why Am I Grown So Cold? Poems of the Unknowable, edited by Myra
Cohn Livingston. Atheneum, 1982.
Poems dealing with the supernatural. **EA LA**

Science and Nature

Arctic Dreams: Imagination and Desire in a Northern Landscape, Barry Lopez. Scribner, 1986. Bantam, paper.

A beautiful, imaginative book on the power of nature and imagination.   **LA**

Cosmos, Carl Sagan. Random House, 1980. Ballantine, paper.

A beautiful book about the galaxy, based on a PBS television series.   **EA LA**

The Lives of a Cell: Notes of a Biology Watcher, Lewis Thomas. Viking, 1974. Penguin, paper.

A biology book that makes science accessible to all readers.   **LA +**

The Medusa and the Snail: More Notes of a Biology Watcher, Lewis Thomas. Bantam, paper, 1987.

Another well written, fascinating book by biologist Thomas. Must reading for budding scientists.   **LA +**

Modern Sports Science, Larry Kettelkamp. Morrow, 1986.

An informative book for student athletes as well as students interested in sports science as a career.   **PA LA**

On the Loose, Terry Russell and Renny Russell. Sierra Club, paper, 1979.

A beautiful book about nature and our responsibility to preserve it.   **EA LA +**

A Passion to Know: 20 Profiles in Science, edited by Allen L. Hammond. Scribner, 1984.

Diverse scientists are discussed in this carefully edited work. A perfect book for students who are considering careers in science.   **PA EA LA**

The Quest for Artificial Intelligence, Dorothy Hinshaw Patent. Harcourt Brace Jovanovich, 1986.

Artificial intelligence is a recent development in computer science. Students interested in other aspects of the computer may enjoy this book.   **EA LA ***

The Riddle of the Dinosaur, John Noble Wilford. Knopf, 1985. Random House, paper.

A Pulitzer Prize winning science writer attempts to solve the riddle of the dinosaur in this thought provoking book.   **EA LA**

The Space Shuttle Story, Luke Begarnie. Scholastic, paper, nd.

An interesting peek inside NASA for preadolescents.   **PA**

A Whale for the Killing, Farley Mowat. Bantam, paper, 1981.

A true account of Mowat's attempt to save a rare fin whale.   **EA LA +**

Whale Watch, Ada Graham and Frank Graham. Delacorte, 1978. Dell, paper.

An interesting account of whaling and whales.   **PA EA ***

The Youngest Science: Notes of a Medicine Watcher, Lewis Thomas. Viking, 1983. Bantam, paper.

Thomas looks back on his own experiences as a medical student.   **PA LA +**

Social Issues

AIDS: In Search of a Killer, Suzanne Levert. Messner, 1987.
    Provides basic information on the virus and two moving accounts of AIDS victims. **LA**

The First Freedom: The Tumultuous History of Free Speech in America, Nat Hentoff. Dutton, 1979. Dell, paper.
    Though this book is now a bit dated, it still gives one of the best historical accounts of the First Amendment right of free speech. **EA LA**

The Great Nuclear Power Debate, Gail K. Haines. Dodd, Mead, 1985.
    Attempts to separate fact from fiction in the nuclear power debate. **EA LA**

Letters to Ms., 1972-1987, edited by Mary Thom. Holt, Rinehart & Winston, 1987.
    These letters chronicle the women's movement from the premier issue of **Ms. Magazine** to 1987. **LA**

Poverty in America, Milton Meltzer. Morrow, 1986.
    A lucid account of reasons for poverty and people who experience it. **EA LA**

The Pulitzer Prizes, Kendall Wills. Simon & Schuster, 1988.
    A collection of Pulitzer Prize winning newspaper articles. **EA LA**

Somebody Else's Kids, Torey L. Hayden. Putnam, 1981. Avon, paper.
    The stories of children rejected by much of society told by their teacher. **EA LA**

South African Dispatches: Letters to My Countrymen, Donald Wood. Holt, Rinehart & Winston, 1987.
    The selections in this book were originally columns in the **Daily Dispatch** published prior to Wood's arrest in 1977. They give a picture of South Africa's people and politics. **LA**

That Mad Game, James Forman. Scribner, 1980.
    An antiwar book that seeks to answer the question of why we have war. **EA LA**

The Tiger Milk: Women of Nicaragua, Adriana Angel and Fiona Macintosh. Holt, Rinehart & Winston, 1987.
    The story of the war torn women of Nicaragua. **LA**

Voices of South Africa: Growing Up in a Troubled Land, Carolyn Meyer. Harcourt Brace Jovanovich, 1986.
    Personal accounts of South Africa told by young people who live there. **PA EA LA**

When and Where I Enter: The Impact of Black Women on Race and Sex in America, Paula Giddings. Bantam, paper, 1985.
    An analytical history of black women activists. **LA**

Sports

Amazing but True Sports Stories, Phyllis Hollander and Zander Hollander.
Scholastic, paper, 1986.
Eighty fascinating sports stories. **PA EA LA**

Even Big Guys Cry, Alex Karras. New American Library, paper, 1978.
A former defensive tackle tells his story. **PA EA LA**

GO! FIGHT! WIN! The NCA Guide for Cheerleaders, Betty Lou Phillips.
Delacorte, 1981. Dell, paper.
A book for cheerleaders and would be cheerleaders that gives advice on how
to make the squad and how to become a champion squad. **PA EA LA**

Grass Roots and Schoolyards: A High School Basketball Anthology, edited
by Nelson Campbell. Viking, paper, 1987.
Stories about high school basketball likely to fascinate adolescents interested
in organized athletics. **EA LA**

Hoosiers, Phil M. Hoose. Ballantine, paper, 1986.
An anecdotal book about basketball madness in Indiana. **EA LA**

The Illustrated Sports Record Book, Zander Hollander and David Schulz.
New American Library, paper, 1975.
A book of records for sports enthusiasts. **PA EA LA ***

The Legend of Dr. J: The Story of Julius Erving, Marty Bell. New American
Library, paper, 1976.
A biography of a great basketball player. **EA LA**

LT: Living on the Edge, Lawrence Taylor and David Falkner. Times, 1987.
A personal account of the life of Lawrence Taylor, New York Giants superstar.
Often shocking and provocative. **LA**

Oh, Baby, I Love It!, Tim McCarver and Ray Robinson. Random House, 1987.
Sportscaster Tim McCarver talks about professional baseball from his
perspective. **EA LA M**

You Are the Coach series, including **Baseball: It's Your Team** (1985); **You Are
the Coach: Basketball** (1983); **You Are the Coach: College Football**
(1985); **You Are the Coach: College Basketball** (1986); **You Are the
Coach: Football** (1983); **You Are the Coach: Hockey** (1984); **You Are
the Manager: Baseball** (1984), Nate Aaseng. Dell, paper.
These books place readers in coaching situations where they must decide the
best move. **PA EA M ***

Survival

Alive, Paul Piers Reed. Lippincott, 1974. Avon, paper.
An exciting true life survival story about a group of soccer players whose
plane crashed in the Andes. **EA LA**

Dove, Robin Graham and L.T. Gill. Harper & Row, 1972. Bantam, paper.
A journal of a 16 year old who sailed his twenty-four foot sloop around the world. **EA LA M**

The Everest Years: A Climber's Life, Chris Bonington. Viking, 1987.
Spectacular photographs accompany this personal, historic quest of Mt. Everest. **EA LA**

Land of the Snow Lion: An Adventure in Tibet, Elaine Brook. Dodd, Mead, 1987.
A personal account of a trek through a remote, off limits area of China. **EA LA F**

Runaway, Lucy Irvine. Random House, 1987.
The author of **Castaway** (Prentice Hall, 1984; Dell, paper) tells about her life prior to her self-imposed island exile. **EA LA F**

The Snow Leopard, Peter Matthiessen. Viking, 1979. Bantam, paper.
An arduous trek through the Himalayas becomes a spiritual pilgrimage. **LA M**

To Fight the Wild, Rod Ansell and Rachel Percy. Harcourt Brace Jovanovich, 1986.
Stranded in Australia's Northern Territory after a boating accident, Ansell used his knowledge of bush lore to save himself. **PA EA M ***

PART THREE

Sharing Books

*T*he art of living cannot be taught or learned by rote, so I believe that we should encourage our children to make inquiry and seek answers, directly, with honesty, through reading and open discussion in the home as well as at school.

Alice Childress

Reading Aloud and Discussing Books

Reading Aloud

Reading aloud is an excellent way to involve the entire family in books. Although many people believe that reading aloud is something done only with small children, the advantages are so great that parents of adolescents should consider building a reading aloud tradition in their families. Before you say "that's impossible," let's discuss why it is so important.

Why Read Aloud?

Earlier in this century, many families gathered in the evenings to listen to one another read. Often the Bible was the primary work shared, but as more books became available families shared the classic works of literature. After the advent of radio and television, the practice of reading aloud became increasingly rare. In recent years educators have begun to understand the tragedy of this loss. Jim Trelease's *The Read-Aloud Handbook* and similar books have encouraged parents of young children to reexamine their oral reading practices. It is time for parents of adolescents to consider the important benefits of this simple, enjoyable pastime.

One reason to read aloud is that it is fun. Skilled readers can captivate audiences of all ages by reading aloud from carefully selected books. Each listener pictures characters and settings differently, thereby fulfilling individual needs.

There are many educational benefits to reading aloud. It can improve skill in reading and listening, foster positive attitudes toward reading, encourage imagination, develop reading maturity, and help bring a family together.

To improve reading skills. Poor readers often read word for word and are unable to understand what they read. They may have difficulty pronouncing words. Their reading skills usually do not keep up with their intellectual and emotional growth. Listening to books read aloud can help poor readers improve their silent reading skills. They hear books as they were meant to be read, and this serves as a model for them. They hear material that is appropriate to their intellectual and emotional maturity. As they listen, they must recall the details of the story and interpret the author's intent. Poor readers rarely have an opportunity to practice these important skills while they are struggling with silent reading. In all of these ways, listening to a work read orally helps young people strengthen their own reading skills.

To improve listening skills. Hearing books read aloud improves listening skills. Teachers often complain that students are not good listeners and that their attention spans are short. One way to increase attention span is by listening to a book of action, suspense, or humor.

To foster a positive attitude toward reading. Parents who enjoy the experience of reading aloud to their family create positive reading models. Readers who have negative attitudes toward reading are likely to have difficulty reading and understanding what they read.

At some time, all of us have experienced personal attitude problems. Perhaps you have taken a course you did not want to take. Every time you picked up the book to study, you found your mind wandering. Overcoming a negative attitude is the first step to reading and understanding. The same is true for adolescents.

For some adolescents, a book they hear read aloud is the first book they have "read" all the way through. The sense of accomplishment that comes from reading an entire book, even if it is read to the adolescent, can be enough to create a positive attitude toward reading. For others, an oral reading selection might be the first book of suspense, fantasy, humor, or science fiction they have enjoyed. The experience may open new reading doors. Listening to a new author for the first time may make a listener search for more books by the same author.

We know that immature readers are more likely to select familiar books than totally new books. Many young readers read the same book repeatedly. The reading aloud experience may give adolescents new books, new authors, and new genres to explore. Reading aloud expands reading horizons.

To foster imagination. Teenagers who watch a great deal of television may lose their ability to create images. Studies have found that typical children watch between six and eight hours of TV per day. Television creates images, reading requires readers to create their own images.

Listening to stories and books read orally helps young people develop their ability to imagine. Characters and places take shape in listeners' imaginations. The importance of imagination cannot be underestimated. A person who cannot create images cannot read because reading requires taking symbols and letters from a page and turning them into words and sentences to create an image. Hearing books read aloud helps adolescents move from the artificial images of TV to more demanding reading material that requires a well developed ability to imagine.

To develop reading maturity. Reading aloud allows adults to share stories with youngsters who do not yet read well enough to read them on their own. Adolescents can participate when great works of literature are read orally. The reader's inflection and emphasis allow the adolescent to put meaning to words and stories too complex for silent reading.

My observation of young readers convinces me that reading maturity develops in most avid silent readers, as well as in those who have been read to. However, it does not develop as rapidly in youngsters who have not been read to on a regular basis. There are two reasons for this. First, adults who read aloud usually select exceptionally well written books with good plots and good characterization. As they listen, youngsters begin to gain a taste for this type of literature. Often adolescents would not discover these books on their own. Second, the language of books often is more impressive when read aloud than when read silently. Good readers often skim books they read silently, losing the subtlety of the author's language and style. Poor readers, on the other hand, may be unable to hear the language as they struggle to understand what the author is saying. Language is central to the experience of listening.

To encourage family togetherness. Recently I overheard a group of middle and high school teachers discussing their students' home lives. A major concern was how little time adolescents spent with their families. Several teachers said it was not unusual for their students to go home to an empty house, eat a sandwich, then go to work. The household with two working parents is the norm rather than the exception. Many adolescents are involved in after school activities or have jobs. Busy schedules prevent families from eating meals together.

All of us recognize the potential problems that arise when communication between parents and youngsters is limited to only a few minutes a day. Recent statistics show that on the average parents talk to their children twelve minutes per day, ten of which are filled with instructions and directions.

Many adolescents find speaking to their parents difficult, and parents experience similar frustration. However, there is no more important time than adolescence to keep the lines of communication open.

Not all families grow apart during the years children are adolescents; many strengthen their relationships. The key to improved relationships appears to be the time that each family member, including adolescents, commits to the family: evening meals, common activities, vacations. Even when time is reserved, communication is not always open. Reading aloud together can open up new lines of communication between parents and adolescents.

A Family Read Aloud Program

If your family does not normally read together, here is a simple plan for beginning a read aloud program.

A good place to get into the oral reading habit is on a long car trip. If you can locate a good book about the place you are going to visit, reading it aloud in the car is natural. The ensuing conversation makes the miles speed by. If a book about your destination is not available, you might read about just one part of your trip, such as a zoo or aquarium.

Of course, the book need not deal with the vacation. It could be one of general family interest. On one of my family's most relaxing, enjoyable vacations we read Richard Adams' *Watership Down*, a book written to be read aloud. In fact, it is based on stories the author told his children as they traveled through Great Britain.

Holidays and birthdays are natural times to begin a reading aloud tradition. We have friends who each select a special poem to read at the birthday dinner of the celebrant. The tradition began when the parents were first married and continued with the birth of each of their children.

Holidays are made for traditions, particularly Christmas and Hanukkah. There are thousands of stories and poems available for these occasions. It's fun for different family members to select at least one new story or poem each year. Several years ago I found Barbara Robinson's hilariously funny *The Best Christmas Pageant Ever*. We enjoyed it so much that each Christmas since we have read it again.

Building a Family Read Aloud Tradition

Once a family read aloud tradition is begun, it is easy to continue. Since the initial experience was enjoyable, it is natural to suggest that it continue on a regular basis.

The key to making a family oral reading time successful is to do it regularly. Reading aloud is habit forming; once the habit is formed, it is hard to break. But first, the family must agree on an appropriate time for reading, a time convenient for all family members. Once the time is set, each family member must reserve that time. If one consistently misses the reading time, others will do the same.

After the time has been set, the first book should be chosen jointly, or the family should agree that the first reader be given the privilege of selecting a book. Choosing a book that is appropriate for the entire family is very important. Try to observe these guidelines.

- Select the book jointly or allow the reader to select a book.
- Be sure the book is appropriate for the reader's skill and the listeners' interest.
- Select a book with a fast paced plot. Look at the first few paragraphs. Are you immediately caught up in the story?
- Select a book with well rounded characters who develop with the story. Be sure listeners can identify with the characters.
- Dialogue should be easy to read. Avoid dialect that is not natural to the reader.
- Select a book with few descriptive passages, at least initially.
- If either reader or listeners are not enjoying the book after the first reading, find a different book.

Reading the Book

If possible, the reader should preread the book; often the most successful read aloud book is one the reader loves. It is much easier to read aloud a book you enjoy than one you do not. If, however, you select a book with which you are unfamiliar and decide after the first oral reading session that you are not comfortable with it, choose another book. In my family, books are not always preread. After the first reading we make a joint decision about whether to continue. Reading aloud should be a pleasure, not a struggle. If readers or listeners are not enjoying a book, stop reading it.

All members of the family should have an opportunity to read or to select a book to be read. One reader should read the entire book. If younger readers are uncomfortable reading an entire book they might select a short story or poem.

All family members should be involved in oral reading. It is often difficult for young children to sit still, so the reading time should be adjusted to their needs. They can be given paper and crayons to illustrate the story as they listen. Even young children should be encouraged to select books they want read. If children are too young to be a regular part of reading sessions, they can be the focus of it when appropriate material is read. Younger members of the family provide a wonderful audience for adolescent readers, who can select books specifically for their younger siblings.

Finding a Location for Reading Aloud

Read aloud sessions should be held in a comfortable place. The reader needs to have a comfortable chair and good light. Listeners should be comfortable and in a position to see and hear the reader. The location should be selected to ensure a minimum of interruptions. Reading outside may seem ideal, but a barking dog or a buzzing bee can be an annoying distraction. If you select a time when there are numerous phone calls, you might want to take the phone off the hook. Constant interruptions limit the pleasure of the experience.

Discussing Books

Books read aloud can inspire parent/adolescent discussions. Talking about incidents, characters, problems, and relationships in books can be a natural way to begin a discussion about important, difficult to discuss issues. Parents and children who have been talking about books for years find the transition from discussing children's books to discussing young adult books quite easy. However, parents who are just beginning to discuss books with adolescents may find that they resist attempts at discussion. It is important that the discussion occur as naturally as possible.

Discussion is impossible unless there is something to discuss. Books read together, either orally or silently, can fill that need. Consider the following points as you plan for book discussions.

- Books should relate to common interests of parents and adolescents.
- Avoid books on topics within the parent's area of expertise. (Adolescents cannot discuss such topics on an equal basis.)
- Nonfiction books in areas of the adolescent's expertise are a good choice.
- Try to choose a type of book that interests the adolescent (mystery, science fiction, adventure).
- The adolescent's favorite book is a good beginning point for discussion.
- Books by an author the adolescent has previously enjoyed are a good choice.
- Initially, avoid books on controversial topics or issues with which you and your teenager do not agree.
- Books should be worth discussing.

How to Discuss a Book

Discussion should flow naturally from common interests and concerns. This is easiest when the book is within an area of new interest for both parent and adolescent.

Allow the adolescent to be the expert. If the book is in an area about which you know a lot, be careful not to preach. Initiate the discussion by allowing the adolescent to take control. For example, suppose your daughter is interested in cooking. You are a gourmet cook, so you suggest a particular cookbook to her. She reads it but doesn't say anything about it. You initiate a discussion by asking, "What did you think of his approach to baking bread?" She answers, "You never make bread without yeast, Mom." She is recognizing your expertise. "I know," you answer, "I've been afraid to try something new, but I'd like to. Would you help me?" You have found an area in which she can be the expert (or at least more nearly equal).

Don't force the discussion. Discussions should not be forced, but the questions you pose must lead to more than simple "yes" or "no" answers. You and your son have read Lois Duncan's *Killing Mr. Griffin.* You ask him, "What did you think of the book?" He says, "It was OK." Not a lot of room for discussion here. Try a new tack. "At first I thought Mark was a bit unrealistic, but then I remembered a kid in my high school class who could convince anyone to do anything." This simple comment might produce, "Yeah, there's a kid in my class like that." Or, it might produce silence.

Try again. "What do you think? Are there really people like Mark?" If he answers with grunts, don't attempt to force the discussion. Wait. He may mention the book later, or maybe he didn't find anything in it worth discussing.

Encourage the adolescent to take the lead as often as possible. If you know your son has some knowledge that might lead to a good discussion of *Killing Mr. Griffin,* begin by encouraging him to use his knowledge. "Aren't you taking psychology this year? Did you study psychotic behavior? Is Duncan's characterization of a psychotic accurate?"

Remain open to the adolescent's opinions. Avoid being judgmental, but encourage clarification. Your son answers, "It was a dumb book." You respond, "Why do you think so? Do you think Duncan's portrayal of Mark was inaccurate?" Many teenagers have learned how to cut off conversations with adults by making what appear to be dead end comments. Try to open all avenues by asking questions that require justification. At the same time avoid getting angry and saying things like, "How could you say that?"

Be honest. Let the adolescent take the lead, expressing opinions and justifying them. If you disagree, simply state your disagreement and explain why, but respect your adolescent's opinion. You say, "I disagree with you on that point. I think there are personalities like Mark. There's a guy in my office who is a lot like Mark. What do you think? Am I way off base here?"

Don't push uncomfortable subjects. Avoid controversial or embarrassing subjects addressed in the book. If the discussion is going well, bring them up when you are both comfortable in the conversation. Don't push the adolescent, but do not avoid topics that need to be discussed. Be patient. If you have successfully opened the lines of communication, it will be much easier to bring up these topics later. You and your son have been discussing the character of Mark on and off for several days. On several occasions he has initiated the discussion. "See that kid over there? He's the one I told you is sort of like a Mark personality." You are concerned about the things you hear some of the kids saying about their teachers. You say, "One thing that really bothered me is that it seemed acceptable for those kids to be so mean to Mr. Griffin. Not one of the kids ever came to his defense. Surely some of them saw some virtue in what he was doing. I've come to respect some of the teachers I thought were mean when I was a kid." Leave plenty of room for him to enter the conversation. Perhaps he will express some similar concerns. If he doesn't, don't push. Sometimes just mentioning the topic is enough.

Treat the adolescent as a discussion equal. Throughout discussions with the adolescent you must assume the same role as do authors of young adult books. Allow the teen to come to his or her own decision. Ask good questions, but avoid giving answers. Be careful not to talk down. Be honest in expressing your opinions, and justify them in the same way you expect the young adult to justify opinions. Be sensitive to the needs of the adolescent.

Discuss books you haven't read. Encourage your teenager to discuss books with you even if you haven't read them. Ask "What are you reading? What's it about?" If your adolescent brings up an interesting topic, you might interject information about a book you have read on a similar topic.

How to Begin a Discussion about a Book

- Initiate the discussion; don't wait for the adolescent to do so.
- Select a common area of interest in which you are *not* an expert.
- Avoid questions that lead to "yes" or "no" answers.
- Avoid judgmental comments about the book or the teen's opinions. Make comments that open doors for further discussion.
- Ask questions that encourage the expressing of an opinion. Avoid giving answers.
- Encourage the adolescent to take the lead in the discussion; select an area of his/her expertise to discuss.
- Remain open to the adolescent's opinions, but ask for clarification and justification.
- Honestly express your own opinions. Be careful not to cut off differing opinions.
- Initially, avoid controversial or embarrassing subjects.
- Be patient, don't push, avoid getting angry.

Conclusion

Reading aloud as a family and discussing topics based on reading can improve communication between parents and adolescents. Communication gaps are caused by lack of time spent communicating rather than by inherent differences. Parents who keep the lines of communication open by sharing common interests are likely to better understand the problems of the young and to narrow the generation gap.

Chapter 9

(Commenting on the release of the American hostages held by Iran)

I sn't it interesting that with all the marvelous computerized and transistorized accomplishments of TV we've yet to hear any of the hostages say, "Thank God we had TV! It got us through our darkest hours. We could never have survived without it."

Jim Trelease

The Electronic Age and Reading

The Influence of Television

Television is a paradox. By the time they finish high school, most students have spent more time watching TV than they have spent on anything else except sleeping. Television (including cable TV and videocassettes) is our most frequent form of entertainment. It is the great equalizer; our access to it has little to do with our economic, social, or educational status. It shapes our lives.

And yet, we condemn television. We call it boring, stupid, simplistic. We blame it for children's reading problems and lack of attention in school, broken families, overemphasis on sports, and even violence. Why?

Television can be destructive, but only if we allow it to be. Almost all studies of television have concluded that it can be a positive force when viewers actively select what they view. Parents must teach children how to control TV, rather than allowing TV to control them. How?

Making Television a Literacy Experience

If we limit access to television and select programs carefully, TV viewing can encourage adolescents to read. Hamilton conducted a study in which junior high school students were given a choice between reading books related to TV programs or reading other books. More than two-thirds of the students selected the television related books. Likewise, 89 percent of students in a Virginia study said they had been influenced to read a book by its related television program. Other studies have found that television is more likely to motivate youngsters to read books than are teachers, parents, or peers.

Parents, teachers, and librarians can use this interest in and enjoyment of television to get young people to read. To do this we must overcome our bias against TV and learn to make it work for us. Among other things, this means we must become selective viewers, limiting the amount of television we watch.

Book Tie Ins

The television and publishing industries have begun to capitalize on television's ability to influence reading by producing media tie ins, a term used to describe books related to media. The tie ins take several forms: TV shows or movies based on books; books based on scripts; books about media celebrities, special events, development of a TV series, and the subjects treated in TV shows; and the actual scripts of television shows and movies.

The three major networks are involved in book/television tie in programs.[1] ABC is attempting to use TV to channel interest toward learning by providing educational materials to schools for use in conjunction with special programs. "After School Specials" and "Weekend Specials" often are based on young adult books.

The CBS/Library of Congress television reading project "Read More About It" features television personalities who mention books related to a program in which they have appeared.

NBC sponsors Parent Participation Workshops—programs that show parents how to lead young people from television to reading to active participation in life. NBC also has tie ins during its "Special Treat" series. At the end of book based programs, stars from the show talk briefly about the book.

In addition to special programing for children and young adults, all the networks present prime time programing based on books appropriate for adolescents. In fact, many young adult books have been the basis for prime time movies.

---

[1]Information about tie in programs is available from the three major networks.

ABC Community Relations, ABC-TV, 1330 Avenue of the Americas, New York, NY 10019-5402

CBS Television Reading Program, 51 West 52 Street, New York, NY 10019-6101

NBC Parent Participation Workshops, Teachers Guide to Television, 699 Madison Avenue, New York, NY 10021

The Public Broadcasting System (PBS) has single shows and series based on books. "Masterpiece Theatre" is known for its literary presentation of classic works. "Wonderworks" presents programing based on children's and young adult books of high quality. If parents watch these shows with their adolescents, they can encourage them to read the book on which the show is based. If parents read the books too, many worthwhile discussions can result. Schools and libraries receive free information and teaching guides on these programs. Parents can get more information from schools or libraries.[2]

News and Documentaries

News and documentaries are useful for obtaining a quick overview of a subject or issue. Adolescents who are encouraged to watch appropriate news and documentary programs often develop an interest in the subject or issue discussed. I have a friend whose professional interest in aquatic biology began with watching Jacques Cousteau underwater exploration programs. Many programs of this type recommend additional reading. Sometimes transcripts of the programs are available for a small charge and bibliographies are provided.

How to Make Television Work for Your Family

- Limit the number of hours television is watched.
- Encourage selective viewing.
  - Plan weekly TV viewing by selecting programs carefully. (Consult television listings for help in planning your viewing.)
  - Seek information from libraries or schools about shows of educational value or book tie ins.
  - Seek shows of high quality and high entertainment value.
- Obtain books related to the shows you plan to watch. (Some school and public libraries do weekly or monthly displays of books related to television programs.)
- If possible, read the book prior to watching the show.
- Recommend appropriate books to adolescents.
- Try to watch shows as a family and discuss them afterwards.
- If you watch quiz shows, watch those with educational value. Play along with contestants.

---

[2]Additional information can be obtained from

Action for Children's Television, 46 Austin Street, Newtonville, MA 02160

Parent-Teacher's Association, 700 N. Rush Street, Chicago, IL 60611

Prime-Time, 120 S. LaSalle Street, Chicago, IL 60603

National Council for Children and Television, 20 Nassau Street, Princeton, NJ 08540

- Allow adolescents to select some popular television shows. Keep in mind how essential peer acceptance is to adolescents. Watch these shows with them and discuss the issues involved.
- Sporting events can lead to good reading. Check your public library for books about sports.
- Check for presentations of high quality motion pictures.
- Watch for details in the program: Is it shot on location? Is the setting appropriate? Are the props appropriate for the time or location? If you have read the book, do you agree with the way characters are portrayed? How does the script differ from the book? Be a critical viewer and encourage the adolescent to be the same.
- Examine news programs for bias. Are all sides of an issue presented? How much time is given to a particular story? Does the report appear to be accurate? Do the pictures go along with the account? Are sources given? Are they reliable?
- Avoid having the television on as background noise. Avoid watching it during dinner. Don't use it as a substitute for real communication.
- Be a model television viewer. If you watch six to eight hours of television a day, your adolescent will probably do the same.

Subscription Television and Videocassettes

Cable television, subscription TV, and videocassettes have changed the way Americans watch television. Television shows can be recorded and watched at another time. Families who subscribe to cable television can view recent motion pictures at home. These new technologies give families more flexibility in terms of viewing choice and time.

Favorite television programs can be recorded, then watched at a time convenient for the entire family. You might choose to record a program at the same time you are watching another program on a different channel. Both of these practices have the danger of increasing the number of hours of television viewing. However, if families are selective, these practices can broaden the scope of viewing possibilities.

Many families are discovering that renting movies on videocassettes increases viewing options. Parents can select films of interest to the entire family. Many films are wonderful entertainment and discussion starters that can lead to new reading interests or open channels of communication between parents and adolescents.

Paid subscription television also broadens the range of television viewing. New networks featuring sports, news, and religious programing are available in many areas. As with videocassettes, this broad range of choice can have a positive effect on family viewing. Parents need to teach adolescents to select their viewing carefully.

The Computer as a Literacy Aid

Many adolescents are familiar with computers used as an entertainment option and an educational tool. Many schools have computers and an increasing number of families have computers at home. An interest in computers can lead adolescents to many magazines and books on computing, computer games, and various aspects of computer technology.

Computers Can Encourage Reading and Writing

Computers offer many possibilities for reading beyond books and magazines about computers. An exciting new trend in computer software is computer fiction. Text based, interactive fiction is available from at least a dozen companies for almost every computer. The fiction is interactive in that readers not only read the story but interact with it by using the keyboard. For example, readers can alter the plot of the story to determine what will happen next. The story proceeds based on readers' responses. In most text based software, readers are not limited to three or four choices but can type almost anything that logically fits the storyline and character development. The only limitation is that the programer must have anticipated the readers' instructions.

Most of the plots currently available are adventure, fantasy, or science fiction. The stories take on the characteristics of a game as readers attempt to extricate the hero from various situations. Many of the stories are based on fiction available in traditional book form. Adolescents who become fascinated with a particular program will probably want to read the book on which it is based. Some of these stories have been adapted to the computer by the authors of the original books, some by computer programers, and some by writers who are hired to turn the books into computer adventure games. Consequently, many of the programs are true to their literary form; readers are rewarded in the program for selecting options that are appropriate to the characters and the plot. Readers must comprehend the author's literary techniques in order to do well in the game.

Interactive fiction is not true literature, but it does use literary techniques and requires the reader's involvement in the story. Adolescents' active involvement in computer fiction may transfer to their reading and writing. Since active involvement with the characters and plot is necessary to comprehend a traditional piece of fiction, the skills learned in playing the game may help readers improve their ability to comprehend what they read. Likewise, computer fiction can help adolescents understand literary techniques used by writers; for example, writers must remain consistent in the development of characters.

Interactive computer fiction is a relatively recent phenomenon. It is still being perfected. The best programs allow almost unlimited choice. Programs that are more literary are better than those that are simply games. The more literary the program, the more likely it is to use techniques adolescents will need when they read a novel or short story and the more likely it is to encourage the adolescent to read the book on which it is based.

The programs contain varying amounts of graphic representation. Though the graphic representation is not essential to the game, it does make it more interesting for many adolescents. It is important that graphics be faithful to the plot, characters, and setting. Programs with limited graphics have a greater potential to help adolescents develop their own imaginations. As in books without illustrations, young readers must imagine the characters and settings when they are not provided by program graphics.

Parents of adolescents who are interested in computers may find these programs a useful way to move adolescents from the keyboard to books. Most computers, however, are considerably more expensive than books. Because of their price and varying quality, it is important that parents examine them carefully for their literary quality, number of options, and potential to move adolescents into books.

Conclusion

I have many concerns about the negative effect of the electronic media on adolescents, but I realize that these concerns come from misuse of the media rather than the media themselves. Used effectively, TV can be a marvelous entertainment and educational tool. It can lead adolescents to books. The same is true of movies and computers.

We have a responsibility to teach young people to use electronic media to their benefit. We must tell adolescents about the potential advantages and disadvantages of TV, movies, and computers. We must be models for our children.

PART FOUR

Locating Books

I believe that [adolescents] are better judges of what constitutes a "good" book than adults. [They] care nothing about best seller lists, what book has won an award and which one has not. [They] know what they like and they read it—not once, but a half dozen times or more.

Jeannette H. Eyerly

Selecting Books

Selecting Books for Adolescents

Selecting books can be difficult. How many times have you gone to a bookstore or library planning to buy or borrow a book and come away empty handed? Sometimes there are too many books to choose from and not enough time to explore them thoroughly; sometimes nothing looks interesting.

Avid adult readers find ways to deal with the problem of too much or too little to read. We have many selection techniques. We may ask advice from friends, librarians, or salespeople in bookstores. Some people read book reviews in newspapers or magazines. Others belong to book clubs. We may read everything we can find by a favorite author or in a favorite genre. Avid adult readers find ways to locate books they are likely to enjoy.

Adolescents often have not developed these skills, so they may select inappropriate books. Teenagers who are unable to find enjoyable books sometimes quit reading. Some adolescents become stuck in a particular kind of book or in books by a particular author because they have not discovered appealing alternatives. Adolescents stuck in a reading rut usually become bored and read less.

Required Reading Can Be Counterproductive

We like to think that adolescents develop reading interest in school, and some do. But since adolescents may not enjoy the books they are assigned to read, required reading does little to build reading interest. If students are permitted to select books to read, they may not be given any guidance in how to select books. Even if they do receive guidance, it may not be helpful. For example, some high school teachers would like all of their students to read the classics, but many young readers are not developmentally ready to read the classics and cannot see themselves on the pages of the book. Even if they are willing to read the required book, requiring specific books does not help them find books on their own for pleasure reading.

Parents Can Help

If adolescents are unable to select books on their own, they will not develop into mature readers. In fact, they may quit reading. Parents must become involved in adolescents' book selections. The first step is knowing which books adolescents will enjoy.

If adolescents have not developed the ability to select books on their own, parents can help by selecting books for them. However, the vast number of available books can frustrate us. Reading the books, visiting the library to keep up with new acquisitions, or checking bookstores on a regular basis is too time consuming for most parents, so we must use some of the same tools we use in selecting books for ourselves. The following guidelines may help.

A Guide to Selecting Books for Adolescents

- Using the book lists in Chapters 6 and 7 as a guide, check local bookstores and libraries to determine the best source of books.
- Keep in mind your adolescent's interests, favorite television shows, and the kinds of books he or she has selected in the past.
- Examine books to determine if your adolescent will find them interesting.
- Make an honest evaluation of how well your teenager reads.
- Ask a young adult librarian, a knowledgeable bookstore clerk, or a teacher for help in selecting books.
- Ask your child's friends what they are reading.
- Enroll your adolescent in a young adult book club.
- Examine books to determine if they are too hard or too easy. (As a rule, easier books have shorter sentences, words, paragraphs, and chapters.)
- Estimate the age of the main character in the book. Most adolescents prefer books with characters slightly older than they are.
- Select three very different books to borrow from the library. They should all be books your adolescent is capable of reading, that deal with his or her interests, and that are like books he or she has selected in the past. Then ask your adolescent to choose a favorite.

- Avoid falling into the trap of saying, "This is a book I would have liked at your age."
- Respect your youngster's choice from the books you selected. Use this choice to guide you in selecting or purchasing the next book.
- As time goes on, select *slightly* more demanding books of higher literary quality.
- In time, select books within parallel genres. (For example, if the teenager likes romances, move to historical romance.)
- Don't push; be patient.
- Encourage your adolescent to select books without your help.

Encouraging Self-Selection

Eventually, selecting books for adolescents becomes counterproductive. They may begin to rely on parents' selections and fail to develop their own selection skills. To avoid this, we must help adolescents become confident in their ability to select books. This confidence is central to becoming a mature reader.

A Guide to Helping Adolescents Select Their Own Books

- Make sure adolescents visit the public library and bookstores regularly.
- Be sure the library and bookstores visited are ones in which adolescents are treated with respect. For example, if the young adult section of your public library is in the children's room, adolescents may be humiliated to be seen there. Express your concern about this to the head of the library.
- Be sure adolescents know where they can find appropriate books in the library or bookstore. (Don't take your teen to the location; be specific in explaining where to find the books.)
- Discuss with adolescents the best bookstores for finding good young adult books.
- Introduce adolescents to librarians and bookstore clerks who know young adult books.
- When you and your adolescent are with her or his friends, ask them about the books they read and enjoy.
- Encourage adolescents to purchase books from school book fairs and school book clubs and to join a young adult book club. (See Chapter 12 for more information.)
- Purchase an annotated bibliography for your adolescents and share Chapters 6 and 7 of this book with them. Encourage them to use these sources in making selections.
- Discuss books of all kinds with the adolescent. (See Chapter 8 for discussion hints.)
- Suggest books or authors you think adolescents might enjoy.
- Respect your adolescent's choices.

Annotated Books and Book Lists

Two valuable books published by the National Council of Teachers of English (1111 Kenyon Road, Urbana, Illinois 61801) help adolescents select their own books. *Books for You*, written for high school students to use on their own, also is a useful source for parents. Nearly 1,200 books of high literary quality, of interest to teenage readers, are annotated. *Your Reading*, designed to be used by middle and junior high school students, annotates over 3,000 books published within an eight year period.

Many organizations update and publish reading lists of books for young adults. These lists usually annotate twenty to thirty recently published books recommended for adolescents, and are available free or for a small charge. Most of the organizations require that you include with your request a stamped, self-addressed envelope. Several lists to write for include: "Best Books for Young Adults," Young Adult Services Division, American Library Association, 50 East Huron Street, Chicago, Illinois 60611; "Books for Young Adults," N231 Lindquist Center, University of Iowa, Iowa City, Iowa 52242; and "Books for the Teenager," The New York Public Library, Office of Branch Libraries, 455 Fifth Avenue, New York, New York 10016.

In addition, the International Reading Association (Box 8139, Newark, Delaware 19714) publishes "Young Adults' Choices," an annotated book list that is updated annually. Books on the list are selected by teenage readers. Single copies are free, but requests must include a self-addressed envelope stamped with two ounces of first class postage.

Conclusion

The best way to assist adolescents in selecting reading material is to be a model. As adolescents observe the selection procedures of influential adults they begin to transfer the techniques to their own book selection.

Like adult readers, young adults usually act on reading suggestions from friends, but parents and teachers also are influential.

The best way to be a valuable resource in the reading selections of adolescents is by knowing what they will enjoy reading. We can do this by being aware of their reading interests and matching these interests to books at appropriate reading levels. It is essential that we assist adolescents in learning to select their own books by developing an environment in which reading and books are central.

The task is not easy, but our influence and guidance may help adolescents become mature readers who appreciate fine literature.

Chapter 11

*R*ead. . . and you will discover a new world of wonder
where librarians will provide you with the magic key to
the best friends you could ever have — books.

Lee Hadley and Ann Irwin

Borrowing Books

Why Borrow Books?

The only way to become a reader is to read books and other materials that meet many needs and address many interests. Adolescents need books to read for pleasure, informational sources containing material for research projects, magazines to help keep their interests current, dictionaries and almanacs, newspapers, and many other types of reading materials.

One of our major responsibilities as parents is to provide an environment in which books are plentiful, but purchasing the vast array of books required by adolescents is impossible. Many books must be borrowed from libraries.

Using the Public Library

Public libraries allow everyone to borrow books, films, audio and videocassettes, magazines, and other materials. Unfortunately, many people do not take advantage of this free resource.

Almost every town has a public library. Most libraries have separate sections for children and many have separate sections for adolescents. If there is no public library in your area, there are probably other sources from which to borrow books. Bookmobiles visit smaller communities on a regular basis. Many small communities have branch libraries or reading rooms from which readers can borrow books. If you are unsure whether these services exist in your area, you can call the nearest public library and ask how it serves your community.

Services for Adolescents

Many libraries have special rroms or sections for children's books. Because adolescents are uncomfortable using the children's room and have difficulty locating appropriate books in the adult book section, many libraries now have rooms or sections for young adults.

Often, there is an overlap in material housed in the children's and in the young adult's book sections of the library, but usually material in children's rooms goes through upper elementary school level and material for young adults begins at middle school level.

The best sections for young adults have comfortable areas for pleasure reading, tables for quiet discussion, and carrels for independent study. They are decorated with posters, pictures, and books of interest to adolescents.

Many librarians compile annotated bibliographies on specific topics for parents, adolescents, and teachers. These include publication information, summaries of books, reading and interest levels of books, and other information of interest to young adults.

Many libraries have special programs for adolescents. Some have regular newsletters that list special events such as movies, visits by authors, plays, storytelling sessions, book discussion groups, and writing circles.

All public libraries have reference sections designed to give quick access to large amounts of information. They usually include encyclopedias, dictionaries, atlases, indexes to magazines and newspaper articles, government documents, telephone books, geological surveys and maps, and almanacs.

Most libraries have current magazines and newspapers. The typical library subscribes to several dozen magazines for readers of various ages with varied interests and backgrounds. Many also subscribe to specialized magazines in addition to the local newspaper, a daily paper from the nearest large city, *The New York Times*, *The Wall Street Journal*, and papers from several other large cities. Most large and middle size libraries keep back issues of major papers and some magazines on microfiche. Back issues of magazines or newspapers the library does not receive may be available through interlibrary loan (a computerized system through which one public library can borrow material from another public library), or the library may be willing to purchase them for its collection.

In addition, many public libraries lend records, recordings, slides, filmstrips, movies, videocassettes, art work, toys, and other educational items.

Most public libraries are part of state library systems and have access to services of libraries throughout the state. Computerization has made it easy for librarians to locate books and information not housed in the local library but available through interlibrary loan.

Teaching Young People to Use Libraries

A family visit to the public library is a good way to help all family members become familiar with library services. Getting library cards is simple. Usually, the only thing required is residency in the area the library serves. Even nonresidents can borrow from most libraries by paying a small fee. Most public libraries require adults to sign for cards obtained by minors.

Few schools take students to the public library, so it is up to parents to teach youngsters to use the public library. Adolescents need to know where reference materials are kept, how magazines are shelved and referenced, how to use the card catalog or the computer catalog to find books in the library, where to find books and how to check them out, where to find nonfiction offerings, and which librarian to ask for help. Most adolescents have difficulty locating material in public libraries because they do not know where and how to find it and are unwilling to ask.

Using School Libraries

Studies show that schools that spend the most money on their libraries are likely to have students who score higher on standardized achievement tests and college entrance exams. Because schools are aware of these studies, they strive to make their libraries useful and inviting places. Most schools train their students to use the library.

Because libraries are so important to adolescents' education and reading development, parents may want to use the following checklist to determine if the school library is adequate to meet students' personal and academic needs.

A Checklist of Middle and Junior High School Library Services

Does the middle or junior high school library have these things?

- A wide variety of fiction books (children's, young adult, adult) appropriate for all readers in the school.
- A wide variety of nonfiction books allowing all readers in the school to research a variety of topics.
- A large number of paperbacks for young adults, shelved separately for browsing and borrowing.
- At least three complete sets of encyclopedias.
- Several intermediate, advanced, and adult dictionaries from different publishers.
- Several atlases.
- Several current almanacs, including special interest almanacs (such as sports).

- A wide variety of magazines of interest to the age group (*Teen, Boys' Life*).
- A wide variety of adult general interest magazines (*Sports Illustrated, Time*).
- Several special interest magazines appropriate for research projects (*Smithsonian, American Heritage, National Geographic*).
- Open shelves for current magazines.
- Several years of back issues of magazines most useful in research.
- Easy access to all books and magazines for all students.
- Easily accessible indexes of magazines available in the library.
- A professional library for teachers.
- Several copies of the local newspaper and at least one state and two national newspapers.
- Adequate and comfortable seating for a full class of students.
- Adequate space for individual study and research.
- Displays to make students want to read and learn.
- A policy that encourages students to use the library.
- Good lighting and ventilation.
- A friendly, helpful, and knowledgeable librarian.

High school libraries should contain materials to help students gain the skills to compete in college level work. The following checklist can help parents determine if the high school library's materials, facilities, and services are adequate for adolescents' personal and academic needs.

A Checklist of High School Library Services

Does the high school library have these things?

- A wide variety of fiction (young adult and adult) appropriate for poor to gifted readers.
- A wide variety of nonfiction, written by knowledgeable researchers, in all subject areas taught within the school, on a wide range of reading levels.
- At least four complete sets of encyclopedias from different publishers.
- Many different intermediate, advanced, and adult dictionaries.
- Numerous atlases on all areas of the world.
- Many almanacs, including special interest almanacs.
- A wide variety of reference books about jobs, colleges, authors, historical data, and scientific data.
- College catalogs.
- Open shelves of magazines of interest to teen readers (*Seventeen, Hot Rod*).
- Open shelves of current general interest adult magazines, including those for advanced readers (*The New Yorker, Harper's*).
- Open shelves for current specialized magazines (*Scientific American, Psychology Today*).
- Several copies of the local newspaper, two state newspapers, and three national newspapers.

- At least five years of bound volumes (or microfiche) of magazines important to research in subject areas taught within the school.
- Appropriate indexes for easy access to articles in magazines.
- Easy access to all books, reference materials, and magazines.
- A large selection of paperbacks for both young and older adults, shelved separately for browsing and borrowing.
- A professional section, including books and journals for teachers in all subject areas.
- Adequate and comfortable seating for a full class of students.
- Quiet areas for individual study and research.
- Tables for quiet conversation.
- Access, through cataloging and appropriate equipment, to audiovisual material and computer software.
- Displays that make students want to read and learn.
- A policy that encourages active use of the library.
- Good lighting and ventilation.
- Friendly, helpful, and knowledgeable librarians and staff.

How to Assess a School Library

Parents can use one of these checklists to assess school libraries. Often the best approach is to discuss the library's strengths and weaknesses with a librarian. Many schools have established parent groups or committees for this purpose.

Of course, not all libraries have all the attributes listed, and many have more. The best equipped school libraries have easily accessible video and audio equipment, computers and software, and separate rooms for small class meetings or group study.

Another aspect of libraries—the people who work in them—can be harder for parents to assess. A dedicated, knowledgeable, caring librarian can improve a good library and help to overcome the shortcomings of a poorer library. However, school libraries often are understaffed. In addition, school librarians are expected to be audiovisual experts, book and audiovisual material purchasers, computer technologists, surrogate teachers, and disciplinarians. The time they can spend with individuals may be limited.

Conclusion

The ability to use and enjoy libraries can change adolescents' lives. In libraries they will discover the world of books and equip themselves to compete in education and the adult marketplace. With access to reading materials from public and school libraries, home reading shelves need never be bare.

Chapter 12

O ur goal as writers for [and parents of] the . . . young
is of course to make them inveterate, chronic readers
whose tastes keep pace with their maturity.

Richard Peck

Buying Books

Building a Home Library

The importance of a home library to the development of a lifelong reading habit
cannot be overemphasized. Children who live with books and who watch their parents select and read books from a home library are likely to become adults who read.

What Books Are Essential in a Home Library?

The wider the variety of books, the wider the reading interests adolescents are
likely to develop. Therefore, it is important that home libraries contain a wide variety
of fiction and nonfiction appropriate to the needs, interests, and maturity of all family members. Books should be available throughout the house: cookbooks in the
kitchen; nonfiction in the den, study, or living room; favorite fiction books in bedrooms. Even bathrooms and workshops are appropriate places for books.

If preschoolers have bookshelves in their bedrooms, their libraries are likely to grow and mature with them. Favorite books are retained and more mature books are added. It is important for parents to ensure that this book collection continues into adolescence.

As young people reach preadolescence, their libraries should begin to contain essential reference books. There are some books every home library should have.

Dictionary. Most homes have dictionaries, but some dictionaries are inappropriate for adolescents. The best adult dictionary is too complicated when a teenager says "How can I look it up if I can't spell it?" or "I can never understand the definition."

There are three categories of dictionaries appropriate for the stages of adolescent intellectual development: intermediate dictionaries for preadolescents (ages 10-13), advanced or student dictionaries for early adolescents (ages 13-15), and adult dictionaries for late adolescents (ages 15-18). Intermediate dictionaries contain most words preadolescents need and use. Typically, they have about one-third the entries of adult dictionaries, list fewer definitions per word, use illustrations, are written on a reading level appropriate for the user, and divide words into syllables without giving specific etymologies. Many intermediate dictionaries contain sample sentences to help users understand words. In short, they are easier to use and understand and less intimidating than adult dictionaries.

Advanced or student dictionaries contain words most commonly used by junior and senior high school students. Like intermediate dictionaries, they are easier to use than their adult counterparts. However, they are more complete and adult appearing than intermediate dictionaries. They provide a transition between intermediate and adult dictionaries. Several good intermediate and advanced dictionaries are available.

- *Macmillan Dictionary for Students* (grades 6-11). Macmillan, 1984.
- *Scott, Foresman Intermediate Dictionary*, second edition (grades 5-8). Scott, Foresman, 1978.
- *Scott, Foresman Advanced Dictionary*, second edition (grades 7-12). Scott, Foresman, 1978.
- *Webster's Intermediate Dictionary* (grades 9-12). Merriam-Webster, 1986.
- *Webster's Scholastic Dictionary* (grades 9-12). Airmont.
- *Webster's New World Dictionary: Basic School Edition* (grades 4-8). Prentice Hall, 1976.
- *Webster's New World Dictionary for Young Readers*. Simon & Schuster, nd.
- *Webster's New World Dictionary of the American Language: Student Edition* (grades 9-12). Simon & Schuster, nd.
- *Webster's School Dictionary* (grades 8-12). Merriam-Webster, 1980.

Parents should plan to replace dictionaries every three or four years. By the time adolescents enter high school they are ready to use adult dictionaries to supplement easier intermediate or advanced dictionaries. Though the adult dictionary is not likely to replace intermediate or advanced dictionaries until late in high school, adolescents should have access to a recent edition of an adult dictionary. The following checklist will help you purchase the appropriate dictionary.

A Checklist for Purchasing a Dictionary for Adolescents

- The adolescent will be able to locate words efficiently in this dictionary.
- The adolescent will be able to understand the definitions.
- The print is readable.
- The illustrations or sample sentences make definitions easy to understand.
- The information is neither too complex nor too elementary.
- A pronunciation key, functional labels, inflectional forms, cross references, synonyms, and abbreviations are included.
- The number of words included is adequate for the adolescent's educational needs.
- The aids at the front and back of the dictionary are appropriate for the adolescent's educational and personal needs (spelling rules, forms of address, name pronunciations and derivations, capitals and their states and countries, and punctuation rules).

Encyclopedia. An encyclopedia is an expensive but valuable family investment. An encyclopedia gives adolescents the opportunity to explore many topics. It is an excellent beginning place for research. There are several junior encyclopedias appropriate for pre and early adolescents. They differ from adult encyclopedias in their presentation of information. They tend to be more colorful, contain more pictures, use simple vocabulary and conversational tone, encourage additional investigation, and pose thought provoking questions. Just as with dictionaries, adult encyclopedias may not be helpful to adolescents. Adult encyclopedias may be difficult to use. Younger adolescents find the descriptions complex and the cross referencing cumbersome. There are two frequently recommended junior encyclopedias:

- *Compton's Precyclopedia* (grades 4-10). Encyclopedia Britannica Educational Corporation.
- *World Book Encyclopedia* (grades 4-12). World Book-Childcraft International.

By the time adolescents enter high school an adult encyclopedia is an important study tool. Though the encyclopedia should never be more than the beginning place for research, it can act as an excellent supplement to textbooks in all disciplines. Throughout middle school, junior high, and the early years of high school the junior encyclopedia may be used daily. However, an adult encyclopedia will be used with increasing frequency. Many excellent adult encyclopedias are available. The following checklist will help you select an appropriate encyclopedia for an adolescent.

A Checklist for Purchasing an Encyclopedia

- The adolescent will be able to read and understand the material in the encyclopedia.

- The material is accurate.
- Each entry presents the most essential information.
- The encyclopedia is cross referenced.
- The adolescent can understand the cross referencing.
- The encyclopedia is well written and enjoyable to read.
- Pictures, maps, graphs, and charts are appropriately placed, fully identified, and easy to understand.
- Each entry makes readers want to learn more about the topic.
- The first paragraph of each entry clearly explains the important points of the entry.
- The encyclopedia meets the adolescent's educational and personal needs.
- The material is up to date.
- The encyclopedia can be updated with supplements.
- The encyclopedia is likely to be useful for many years.

Atlas. An atlas should be included in home libraries. Good atlases include more than maps; they are helpful as adolescents study geography, history, and science. *The World Atlas for Students* (Hammond) is particularly good for junior and senior high school students. *Rand McNally Children's Atlas of the World* is slightly less complete; it is better for students in grades four through seven. Atlases that can be used by the whole family include *Rand McNally Family World Atlas* and *Rand McNally Family Adventure Road Atlas*.

As with dictionaries and encyclopedias, adult atlases are often too complicated for adolescents. However, by the time teens reach upper levels of high school, they need specialized information. Therefore, both a student atlas and a complete adult atlas are helpful additions to a home library. This checklist will help you select an appropriate atlas for an adolescent.

A Checklist for Purchasing an Atlas

- Maps include all the regions of the world and are easy to read and understand.
- The atlas contains material at an appropriate maturity level for the adolescent.
- Narrative sections are located near appropriate maps and are easy to read and understand.
- Narratives are neither too complex nor too elementary.
- The atlas has a good index.
- Cross references are easy to locate.
- Supplemental information such as climate, population, agricultural products, and capitals is easy to locate and understand.
- If the atlas is an adult atlas, additional information is included (politically related areas, changes in countries due to war and politics, energy production, trade routes, air connections, surface configuration, natural vegetations).
- Illustrations are accurate and help readers understand the material.
- The material is up to date.

Almanacs are inexpensive resources filled with interesting facts about hundreds of topics. Most are updated annually. All almanacs include a detailed index. The two most popular almanacs for home use are *The Information Please Almanac* (Simon & Schuster) and *The World Almanac and Book of Facts* (Newspaper Enterprises and Doubleday).

Since almanacs are so easy to use, junior versions are rarely necessary. However, annual updating is. If an adolescent is reluctant to take on an adult almanac, you can purchase reasonably priced almanacs devoted to single subjects, such as football. Almanacs designed specifically for young people, such as the *Kids' World Almanac* (Pharos Books), may be enjoyed by pre and early adolescents.

An unusual almanac that almost all adolescents enjoy is the *Guinness Book of World Records*, updated annually (Bantam, paper).

Books for enjoyment. A child's first books usually are purchased by parents, grandparents, or adult friends. Most adults do not hesitate to purchase books for preschool children, but book purchases by adults tend to decrease by the time children reach late elementary school. This is unfortunate since preadolescents frequently have difficulty selecting interesting books.

Books for adolescents need not be expensive. Paperback books for young adults usually cost between $2.25 and $3.50. They cost even less when purchased through book clubs or at used bookstores. Hardcover books for young adults rarely cost more than $13.00.

Since hardcover books will be kept for many years, parents and adolescents should be sure books purchased in hardcover are ones the student wants added to the personal library. I suggest that adolescents who are building personal libraries first borrow hardcover books from the public or school library to be sure these are books they want to read again and again.

Where to Buy Books

Bookstores

There are many types of bookstores. The two most common are locally owned bookstores and bookstore chains. There are major differences in how they select and stock books.

Local bookstores are interested in the reading interests of the local population. They usually stock books from a variety of distributors and publishers. They may not have a large number of copies of a single title, but they are likely to stock a broad range of books. Some specialize in books for young people; others carry only books for adults. Most local bookstores will order books that are not in stock. Local bookstores rarely discount books. However, they are likely to carry a broader range of material than do chain stores.

Chain bookstores are stocked through distribution centers that are concerned about the volume of book sales across the country. Since individuals rarely buy young adult hardcovers, chain bookstores do not stock them and often are unable to order them. Chain bookstores tend to have a large number of individual paperback titles by the most popular authors. If you want a recent young adult paperback, you are likely to find it in a chain bookstore.

Nonbookstore Locations

Best selling young adult books often are sold in supermarkets, drugstores, and discount department stores. Books in these stores are likely to include formula books, television or movie tie in books, and best selling titles.

Used bookstores are good sources for reasonably priced books. Some have a large stock of young adult paperbacks, although they are rarely shelved in separate sections. Therefore, you need to be familiar with specific titles and authors so you recognize them on the shelves.

Libraries sometimes sell books that have not been checked out recently, duplicate copies, or donated books. Often you can purchase these books for a fraction of the original cost.

Book Fairs are another source of paperback books for adolescents. These increasingly popular events are sponsored by a school or a library that invites a distributor to display books for sale. Books tend to be less expensive than in bookstores.

Paperback book clubs are the largest distributors of paperback books for young people in the United States. Most book clubs operate through classrooms. At regular intervals, the book club sends teachers an annotated list of books. Students receive flyers that describe the books and the authors. Students give completed order forms to the teacher, who orders for the group. Premiums are given if enough books are ordered.

Book clubs offer books ranging from classics to comics. Parents should supervise what adolescents order to ensure that they select a wide variety of books, not only those that are most popular with classmates.

Books from book clubs are less expensive than books in bookstores. Since book clubs typically purchase the right to publish a book from the original publisher, the quality of the binding, paper, and illustrations often is inferior to books in bookstores, but this keeps the cost down. Book clubs offer a wonderful opportunity for adolescents to develop a book buying habit.

Some book clubs, notably the Junior Literary Guild, sell hardcover books for adolescents. Members receive books selected by book club editors. This means the books are free from controversy and should appeal to all readers. The Junior Literary Guild features books on three levels: ages 9-10, 11-12, and 12 and up. Selections include fiction and nonfiction titles of general interest. They are sent for a specified monthly charge (plus shipping), considerably below bookstore prices. The major advantages of belonging to a book club are reduced costs and regular book purchases.

The major disadvantage is that members always receive the selected book, whether they want it or not, unless they notify the club before the book is sent.

Many adolescents also can find selections of interest in adult book clubs such as Book of the Month Club and Literary Guild.

Books are included in catalogs from many mail order firms, museums, and department stores. Some mail order firms that specialize in books offer discount prices for books ordered in sets. If you are a member of a book club, you probably receive many of these catalogs. If you'd like to receive them, most mail order firms send catalogs at no charge.

Conclusion

Home libraries are important. Books we haved saved throughout the years are a mark of who we are and what we have become. Personal libraries mature and grow with individuals. Parents and adolescents who are aware of the variety of sources for purchasing books can begin an excellent home library without great cost. Young adults who begin building a home library today will be "inveterate, chronic" readers tomorrow.

Chapter 13

The Fervent Prayer of a Teenager's Parent

O h Higher Power,
       And I wish I were —
              Give me to know that the easier life is made for
the young, the harder they will make it for themselves and each
other.

Harden my heart and stop my ears against what other people
let their kids do.

Strike me dumb when I blame a teacher I have never met, for
heaven alone knows what that teacher has heard about me.

Let not the coach build his career on the vulnerable flesh of
my son.

Spare my daughter the sly pornography of soap operas.

Send summer reading lists so my children won't lose three
months of a fertile growing season.

Sharpen my eye as I ransack my child's room to find and
destroy the fake ID.

Embolden my heart as I unplug the telephone from my child's
room so that the peer group that rules the school all day will not
rule our nights as well.

Stay my hand when I am tempted to buy my children's love
with credit cards in their names, or mine.

Strengthen my spine as I impose a curfew, lest my nights be a
hell of waiting for the fatal phone call.

And give me ears to hear that when the young cry out for
new freedoms, they are demanding old rules. Amen

Richard Peck

Books and Magazines about Adolescents

Locating Material about Adolescents

Some of us dread having our youngsters become teenagers, remembering the difficulties of our adolescence. Some of us, as Louise Kaplan suggests, "have forgotten the painful emotions associated with becoming adult [and] tend to imagine the adolescent years as brimming with opportunity." Either way, we are likely to experience the difficulties of adolescence along with our children.

Unfortunately, help in dealing with adolescents is not easy to find. The number of books for parents of adolescents is a small fraction of those published for parents of infants. However, there are some books that can help us. The following books assist parents in understanding adolescents and suggest ways to make adolescence easier for parents and children.

Books for Parents

After All We've Done for Them: Understanding Adolescent Behavior.
Louis L. Fine. Prentice Hall, 1979.
This easy to read guide helps parents deal with adolescents' problems: peers, drugs, obesity, sexuality, ailments, depression, and divided families.

Between Parent and Teenager. Haim Ginnott. Macmillan, 1969. Avon, paper.
Though a bit dated, this may be the most complete, helpful resource book for parents of teenagers. The book helps parents deal with conflicts with their adult children and gives helpful examples throughout.

Boys and Sex, revised edition. Wardell B. Pomeroy. Delacorte, 1981. Dell, paper.
This book for adolescent boys and their parents discusses the physiological, psychological, and social factors involved in the adolescent male's sexual development. The author stresses the importance of responsibility in healthy sexual maturing. A question and answer section deals with adolescents' common concerns.

Children and Money: A Parent's Guide. Grace W. Weinstein. New American Library, 1987.
A personal finance expert advises parents of children of all ages about helping children learn to spend wisely, save, and acquire money management skills. Topics range from allowances to trusts and wills. A section on teenage spending is particularly helpful.

Coping with Teenage Depression. Kathleen McCoy. New American Library, 1985.
This study of why depression is so widespread and destructive advises parents how to recognize depression and what to do about it.

The Essential AIDS Fact Book: What You Need to Know to Protect Yourself, Your Family, All Your Loved Ones. Paul Harding Douglas and Laura Pinsky. Pocket Books, 1987. An easy to read source of information on AIDS and how to avoid it.

The Family Handbook of Adolescence. John E. Schowalter and Walter R. Anyan. Knopf, 1981.
This medically oriented guide written for parents and teenagers is easy to read and carefully documented. It contains information on physical development, sexual maturation, health, social issues, parental issues, medical care, and physical and psychological problems.

Girls and Sex, revised edition. Wardell B. Pomeroy. Delacorte, 1981. Dell, paper.
This book for adolescent girls and their parents gives accurate information and practical advice about physical and emotional changes related to puberty. The author emphasizes the need for girls to have a comfortable understanding of their sexuality. A question and answer section deals with many common problems.

How to Help Children with Common Problems. Charles E. Schaefer and Howard L. Millman. New American Library, 1982.
Parents are advised about dealing with problems of childhood and adolescence, including shyness, sex, obesity, and drugs.

Kids and Drugs: A Parent's Handbook of Drug Abuse, Prevention, and Treatment. Jason D. Baron. Putnam, 1984.
Symptoms of drug abuse and various treatments are described.

Kids Can Read Better. Victoria Williams. New American Library, 1985.
Ways to improve adolescents' reading in five minutes a day are discussed.

Movie Guide for Puzzled Parents. Lynn Minton. Delacorte, 1985. Dell, paper.
This collection of 1,500 movie reviews deals with the content of movies on TV and videotape. Minton discusses aspects of films that can disturb young people and recommends the ages for which each movie is appropriate.

The New Child Health Encyclopedia. Boston Children's Hospital Staff. Delacorte, 1987. Dell, paper.
This reference book for parents deals with all aspects of children's health.

Not My Kid: A Parent's Guide to Kids and Drugs. Beth Polson and Miller Newton. Avon, 1985.
This is a practical guide to identifying a drug problem and dealing with it.

Raising Sons: Practical Strategies for Single Mothers. Joann Ellison Rodgers and Michael F. Cataldo. New American Library, 1984.
This book for single mothers of sons of all ages helps single mothers develop a flexible system of childrearing. The authors show how to be alert to problems and how to negotiate changes in behavior.

Signals: What Your Child Is Really Telling You. Paul Ackerman and Murray Kappelman. New American Library, 1980.
This book analyzes the problems of childhood and adolescence and the hidden messages they contain. It includes a section on the roles of teachers, pediatricians, and mental health professionals.

What Do You Really Want for Your Children? Wayne Dyer. Avon, 1986.
This is a practical guide for raising healthy, happy, self-reliant, confident children.

Professional Books about Adolescence

Adolescence: The Farewell to Childhood. Louise J. Kaplan. Simon & Schuster, 1984.
This academic but lyrical description of adolescence deals with theories of adolescence and discusses the problems of modern adolescents, including independence versus authority, sexuality, growth spurts, mother-daughter relationships, and father-son relationships.

How Children Fail, revised edition. John Holt. Dell, 1982.
Though this book does not deal specifically with learning problems, it can help parents understand why their children have difficulty in school. Holt suggests many ways to help children learn to their full potential.

How Children Learn, revised edition. John Holt. Delacorte, 1983. Dell, paper.
Holt examines children's learning processes, grades and grading practices, testing, trust, and authority. He challenges the educational system and shows how parents can help their children learn.

My Mother/My Self. Nancy Friday. Dell, 1987.
> A fascinating narrative in which the author explores relationships between mothers and daughters.

A Piaget Primer: How a Child Thinks. Dorothy S. Singer and Tracey A. Revenson. New American Library, 1978.
> This book examines the work and complex theories of developmental psychologist Jean Piaget, who many believe provided the most important insight into how thinking is developed. Though this book does not specifically address adolescence, it can help parents understand adolescents' intellectual development.

Vivienne: The Life and Suicide of an Adolescent Girl. John Mack and Holly Hickler. New American Library, 1982.
> A psychiatrist and an educator attempt to understand what made an intelligent, sensitive 14 year old take her life. This moving book may help parents recognize danger signs in their own children.

Widening Circles. Elizabeth Lyttleton Sturz. Harper & Row, 1983.
> Provides practical guidelines for dealing with young adults who are chronic underachievers, runaways, addicts, or criminals. Based on the work of the South Bronx Argus Learning for Living Center.

Young Girls: A Portrait of Adolescence. Gisela Konopka. Prentice Hall, 1976. Harrington, paper.
> This is a sensitive presentation of an extensive research study on adolescent girls, featuring comments from the girls in the study.

Magazines about Adolescence

The problem of finding current, helpful information about adolescence is probably most evident in magazines. Though there are several academic journals that deal with adolescence, no popular magazines are devoted entirely to the adolescent. The following magazines offer a limited number of helpful articles in each issue.

Children. Rodale Press. Several articles in each issue discuss adolescents and issues related to adolescence. The advisory board includes a specialist in adolescent medicine. There are articles on mental and physical health, media, books, products, computers, and sports.

Parent's Choice. Parent's Choice Foundation. This magazine provides reviews of children's media to alert parents to trends and events in books, TV, records, films, and toys.

Parents' Magazine. This magazine concentrates mostly on younger children, but does include some articles on adolescent behavior and development.

Professional Journals of Interest to Parents

Adolescence. Libra Publishers. This scholarly journal with articles by physicians, psychologists, psychiatrists, sociologists, and educators contains many helpful articles for parents.

ALAN Review. Assembly on Literature for Adolescents-National Council of Teachers of English. This journal contains many reviews of new young adult books, and articles about the books and their authors.

Conclusion

The road to increased understanding is paved with books. Nearly every book written on adolescence begins with a statement about the difficulty of understanding adolescents. F. Phillip Rice begins *The Adolescent* in this way:

Contemporary Western society is ambivalent in its attitudes and feelings toward adolescents. Adolescents are admired, praised, and almost worshiped; they are criticized, belittled, and rejected.

We need books and articles to help us understand what is normal in adolescent development, to help us deal with the problems of adolescence, and to help us feel more adequate as parents of adolescents.

References

Bettelheim, Bruno, and Zelan, Karen. *On learning to read: The child's fascination with meaning.* New York: Knopf, 1982.

Carlsen, G. Robert. *Books and the teenage reader,* second edition. New York: Harper & Row, 1980.

Early, Margaret. Stages in growth and literary appreciation. *English Journal,* March 1960, 161-167.

Edwards, Margaret A. *The fair garden and the swarm of beasts: The library and the young adult.* New York: Hawthorn, 1974.

Ellis, W.G. To tell the truth or at least a little nonfiction. *ALAN Review,* 1987, *14* (2), 39-41.

Gentile, Lance M., and McMillan, Merna M. Why won't teenagers read? *Journal of Reading,* 1977, *20,* 649-654.

Hamilton, H. TV tie-ins as a bridge to books. *Language Arts,* February 1976, 129-130.

Havinghurst, Robert. *Developmental tasks and education,* third edition. New York: David McKay, 1972.

Kaplan, Louise J. *Adolescence: The farewell to childhood.* New York: Simon & Schuster, 1984.

Peck, Richard. Some thoughts on adolescent literature. *News from ALAN,* September-October 1975, 4-7.

Rice, F. Philip. *The adolescent: Development, relationships, and culture,* fifth edition. Boston: Allyn & Bacon, 1987.

Spinelli, Jerry. Before the immaculate cuticles. *ALAN Review,* 1986, *14* (1),15-18.

Trelease, Jim. *The read-aloud handbook,* second edition. New York: Penguin, 1986.

PART FIVE
Appendix

Book Publishers

Atheneum Publishers
115 Fifth Avenue
New York, NY 10003

Atlantic Monthly Press
19 Union Square West
New York, NY 10003

Avon Books
1790 Broadway
New York, NY 10019

Ballantine/Del Rey/Fawcett Books
201 East 50 Street
New York, NY 10022

Bantam Books
666 Fifth Avenue
New York, NY 10103

Bradbury Press
866 Third Avenue
New York, NY 10022

Thomas Y. Crowell
10 East 53 Street
New York, NY 10022

Crown Publishers
225 Park Avenue South
New York, NY 10003

Delacorte Press
One Dag Hammarskjold Plaza
New York, NY 10017

Dell Publishing Company
One Dag Hammarskjold Plaza
New York, NY 10017

Dial Books for Young Readers
2 Park Avenue
New York, NY 10016

Dodd, Mead & Company
71 Fifth Avenue
New York, NY 10003

Doubleday & Company
666 Fifth Avenue
New York, NY 10103

E.P. Dutton
2 Park Avenue
New York, NY 10016

Farrar, Straus & Giroux
19 Union Square West
New York, NY 10003

Four Winds Press
115 Fifth Avenue
New York, NY 10003

Greenwillow Books
105 Madison Avenue
New York, NY 10016

Grosset & Dunlap
51 Madison Avenue
New York, NY 10010

Gulliver Books
1250 Sixth Avenue
San Diego, CA 92101

Harcourt Brace Jovanovich
1250 Sixth Avenue
San Diego, CA 92101

Harper & Row
10 East 53 Street
New York, NY 10022

Holiday House
18 East 53 Street
New York, NY 10022

Henry Holt and Company
113 West 18 Street
New York, NY 10011

Houghton Mifflin Company
One Beacon Street
Boston, MA 02108

Alfred A. Knopf
201 East 50 Street
New York, NY 10022

Lerner Publications Company
241 First Avenue North
Minneapolis, MN 55401

J.B. Lippincott
East Washington Square
Philadelphia, PA 19105

Little, Brown & Company
34 Beacon Street
Boston, MA 02106

Lodestar Books
2 Park Avenue
New York, NY 10016

Lothrop, Lee & Shepard Books
105 Madison Avenue
New York, NY 10016

Macmillan Publishing Company
866 Third Avenue
New York, NY 10022

Margaret K. McElderry Books
866 Third Avenue
New York, NY 10022

Julian Messner
1230 Avenue of the Americas
New York, NY 10020

William Morrow & Company
105 Madison Avenue
New York, NY 10016

New American Library
1633 Broadway
New York, NY 10019

Pantheon Books
201 East 50 Street
New York, NY 10022

Philomel Books
51 Madison Avenue
New York, NY 10010

Pocket Books
1230 Avenue of the Americas
New York, NY 10020

Prentice Hall
1230 Avenue of the Americas
New York, NY 10020

G.P. Putnam's Sons
51 Madison Avenue
New York, NY 10010

Random House
201 East 50 Street
New York, NY 10022

Scholastic
730 Broadway
New York, NY 10003

Charles Scribner's Sons
866 Third Avenue
New York, NY 10022

Viking Penguin
40 West 23 Street
New York, NY 10010

Walker & Company
720 Fifth Avenue
New York, NY 10019

Franklin Watts
387 Park Avenue South
New York, NY 10016